THE INITIATION

THE INITIATION

Donald Schnell

ELEMENT

Boston, Massachusetts • Shaftesbury, Dorset
Melbourne, Victoria

First published in the USA in 2000 by
Element Books, Inc.
160 North Washington Street, 4th Floor
Boston, Massachusetts 02114

Published in Great Britain in 2000 by
Element Books Limited
Shaftesbury, Dorset SP7 8BP

Published in Australia in 2000 by
Element Books Limited for
Penguin Books Australia Limited
487 Maroondah Highway, Ringwood, Victoria 3134

Library of Congress Cataloging-in-Publication data available.

British Library Cataloguing in Publication data available.

Printed and bound in the United States by Edwards Brothers.

ISBN 1-86204-820-7

CONTENTS

ACKNOWLEDGMENTS

I would like to thank my stepdaughter, Lisa Neuwirth, who had the initial vision of this book and labored with Marilyn and me to bring it to the public. Lisa's timely input lifted the project to the next level repeatedly. Her artistry and sensitivity to words are only surpassed by her transcendental chocolate chip cookies.

I would also like to thank my stepson, Greg Neuwirth, who funded the project and was one of the reasons I went to India. Thank you, Greg, for your faith.

My gratitude to my stepson, Beau Diamond, whose upbeat attitude is always an inspiration. Thank you Beau for your example.

To my son Michael: Love.

Most importantly, I dedicate this book to my wife, Marilyn Diamond. Without her love, belief and tireless support for the past seven years, this book would not have "materialized." I can never thank you enough, my darling.

All praise be to you, Babaji. I bow to your lotus feet. May this humble offering from our hearts to your heart bring you a smile.

Love,
Dr. Donald Burton Schnell

FOREWORD

On February 10, 1999, I was looking through my stepfather's archive of floppy discs hoping to find biographical material for a book he was working on, *Journey to Premananda.* When I came across a disc labeled "Babaji," I printed it out, and discovered a 136-page, stream-of-consciousness passage, recounting one extraordinary day of transformation in my stepfather's life.

I read the manuscript three times, and I couldn't put it down. As if propelled by a force beyond myself, I announced to my parents that I wouldn't rest until it was published. For the next week, my mother, my stepfather and I did nothing but work together around the clock. Eight days after I pulled it out of obscurity, on February 18, 1999, "Babaji," part one of *The Initiation* was expressed overnight to our literary agent in New York.

My passion for this book is particularly interesting because I am the skeptic in the family. My stepfather, Dr. Donald Schnell, returned from India exactly one year ago as "Prema Baba Swamiji." The truth is I have been too embarrassed to call him "Swamy," like most of the public does, or "Baba," the name his students use to address him; or Prema (heart), which my mother has adoringly nicknamed him. But after reading this manuscript, I found myself humbly and lovingly addressing the stepfather I've known for seven years as "Baba." You will soon understand why.

When I read this book, I realized that I had forgotten that I was searching. Growing up as Marilyn Diamond's only daughter, I was passionate about everything and *anything* alternative, and grew up in a world of abundant possibilities. I enthusiastically sought an understanding of God, health, philosophy—and dreamed of being an artist or a writer. I did yoga every day and was truly happy. As the years passed, I came to emphasize the "worldly stuff" out of a sense of obligation, and developed an "I've already done the spiritual stuff" attitude. Reading this manuscript woke me up to the fact that I have been distracted, for more than a decade, by my quest for "success."

The truth is that no matter what I have done, I have secretly felt a void within. I was successful professionally, had a lively social life, networked with interesting people in many fields, and traveled extensively. I had a busy, fun life. But I was also frustrated and stressed, and my heart was in turmoil. Why?

Because I wasn't really connected with God.

Like many Gen-X Americans, I have always taken for granted that God lies within. But the truth is I had never learned how to access that higher power. Although I yearned for authentic inspiration, I was unable to figure out how to find it in the day-to-day crush of '90s-style survival. Like so many people, I ended up feeling "burned out." Is an authentic spiritual life really as expensive and complicated as the television commercials and self-help books tell us? I can't afford a week at a retreat. And I can't bear to see one more *Ten Easy Steps to...* on the bestseller list. I've bought many of those books, kicking myself for spending my hard-earned money on something I will never stick to . . . if I ever even read it. On the way home from the bookstore I'd usually stop at Blockbuster, then add the new book to the big pile by my bed, as I popped a cassette into the VCR.

It's easy to become cynical. Everyone—from Hollywood starlets to corporate America yuppies—has something to say about how to make our lives better. And everyone wants it to be quick and easy.

But who can really teach us how to live a balanced, healthy and meaningful life? I never connected with mainstream religion, though I studied various schools of spiritual thought in my teens. I came to think of myself as universal and independent. A child of the new millennium, if you will. "I'll do it my own way. It's a new age. Let's make it up as we go along." Right?

Wrong.

This book brought home to me the fact that the science of living a fulfilling life is nothing new, really. As a matter of fact, it's ancient. Prema Baba Swamiji is a teacher, a leader, a Guru, a spiritual Master. He has carried the ancient wisdom within him since childhood. This book tells the story of his sacred initiation as he was made aware of his role as one who can connect seekers to God.

I believe that *The Initiation* has the power to open minds, and will touch you with the reality of universal love. In sharing his initiation in the tender way he does, Baba has initiated me, too. I am different. I am awake. I again know who I really am. And my dreams suddenly make sense. You'll see.

Lisa Neuwirth

WELCOME TO THE READER

Dear Friend,

Namaste!

This greeting comes from the ancient Sanskrit, the spiritual language of India. In Western terms it means, "as my soul honors yours, I welcome you with all my heart." Implied in the word is the idea that we all share a divine essence that unites, rather than separates, us.

I greet you with *Namaste* to welcome you to a journey into the heartland of India, and beyond. In truth, the journey you are meant to take in this book is to the center of your heart. Once there, you will find *prema*, the love, tenderness and compassion that are the essence of who you *really* are. And you will also find *ananda*, an indescribable bliss, the unlimited joy of the child who lives in the center of your being. This journey to *premananda* comes only to the fortunate. It is the most worthwhile of all journeys, and Prema Baba Swamiji is uniquely qualified to take you there. In my seven years by his side, I've repeatedly seen the most extraordinary spiritual transformations taking place in those he touches. This book has been written to touch *you*. What more can I say? Read it and see what happens.

In the ancient Indian sacred text, the *Guru Gita* ("The Song of the Guru") it is said that the Guru is "the wish-fulfilling tree." If you give your desires and dreams to the Guru, then he, who is closest to God through his devotion, intercedes and takes your prayers to God for you. If your faith is pure and patient, your prayers are answered. Jesus, in the tradition of the Eastern Guru, gave us this model in the West, and many people pray to him. But few in our culture realize that living Gurus walk among us in every age, including this one.

Marilyn Diamond
Co-author, *Fit for Life*

BABAJI

Have you ever heard of Babaji? Many people of the sixties know Babaji as the mysterious figure sitting in lotus posture and floating above all the notables on the cover of the Beatles' *Sergeant Pepper* album. Babaji is known to the spiritual seekers of India as the *deathless Maha-Avatar. Maha* is a Sanskrit descriptor, which literally means "mega." *Avatar*, also Sanskrit, means "the descent of Divinity into flesh." It is recorded that Babaji is the immortal Yogi-Christ/Buddha[1] who works for the spiritual salvation of this age. Although he never openly appears in any century, in India's spiritual legacy it is said that in medieval times Babaji initiated the famous spiritual master Shankara, who then founded the Ancient Order of Swamis.

"*Baba*" means father and "*ji*" indicates reverence. The equivalent in English is Holy Father. The devout believe that when you repeat the name "Babaji" with reverence, you bring a blessing into your life.

Babaji works through the prophets in every era to guide human evolution. His purpose is to inspire you to remove the conditions of war and racial and religious prejudice. Babaji doesn't deny your material goals, whatever they may be. He doesn't care whether you have a Mercedes or a bicycle, whether you live in a grand palace or a trailer. His concern is your spiritual happiness. His vision is a world filled with *prema*, the divine quality of tenderness, love and compassion for one another.

Babaji was first seen in the 1800s when he gave spiritual initiation to Sri Lahiri Mahasaya, a famous Yogi saint. He appeared to Mahasaya's student and to his student Paramahansa Yogananda. Babaji's body shows no signs of age. He continues to look about twenty-four, even though he has lived hundreds and maybe thousands of years.

Spiritual masters who have transcended death are not unique to India. In the West, both Thomas Jefferson and Benjamin Franklin saw Count Saint Germain, who was known to live through the 1500s to the 1800s. Saint Germain made quite an impression on many through his wisdom. Legend tells us that he stunned his private visitors visually by wearing a coat of diamonds. Eventually, he went into hiding, making himself available only to sincere spiritual seekers. Spiritual masters are not keen to satisfy the merely curious, or those seeking sensationalism. Those who want to be entertained by feats of wonder can spend an afternoon at the circus. Masters come to bring blessings, guidance and instruction to advanced souls who have prepared themselves.

These spiritual masters are available to all sincere people. No matter where you live, you can have their blessings and guidance in your life. You can connect to them through the power of meditation. Meditation puts the brain and body into the right frequency to receive the finer spiritual messages and healing vibrations of the masters. When it is your time to receive their benediction, they will reveal themselves to you if you take the appropriate steps to receive them. It is like radio: if you're in the mood for classical music, but your radio is tuned to a rap station, you are not going to receive the music you want to hear.

The only motivation true spiritual masters have in coming to you is to awaken you to your center of divine love. The tradition of universal spirituality taught through prema—unlimited love—reveals certain strategies that will assist you in connecting to the refined energies of your own divinity.

In November 1997, Babaji revealed his physical form to me in India. This event, and everything else that happened in the week that followed, changed my life completely—and made sense of the events of my life that led me to that moment. I had been a student of most things spiritual from early childhood, thirsting for an understanding of my connection to God. I'd studied from the age of seven, longed for the presence of masters in my life, and unusual events I never clearly understood led me to be the student of seven of the great Eastern and Western spiritual Gurus of our era.

I had never consciously sought or even thought of Babaji in many years. However, I clearly recall that as an eight-year-old American child growing up in the Cold War era of the 1960s, I used to pore over the drawing of him in Paramhansa Yogananda's classic *Autobiography of a Yogi*, which I had taken from my father's library. As I filled my consciousness with the image of the long-haired Babaji who appeared so young, sitting bare-chested in a lotus position, I sincerely prayed to him, believing that if I did so, he would respond. It seemed to be true as I felt an inner response. I asked for Babaji's *upadesha*. I knew the word *upadesha* even then—it means spiritual guidance and blessings. Specifically, I prayed that he would appear to me, and I prayed that he would guide my life to make it possible for me to meet him some day.

Forty years later in the fall of 1997, I had long forgotten this prayer, when I answered an urgent call to India from my Guru Sri Sri Swamy Nagananda. The call was so insistent that it awakened me at 6:30 A.M. on November 18. I was in Los Angeles—having returned the night before from a publicity tour in Australia. The moment I opened my eyes, I knew I had to leave for India that very day. I had no ticket, no visa and no traveling clothes suitable for the tropics; but despite visa problems, financial problems and last-minute airline pressures because of holiday traffic, that evening I flew overnight to New York, and departed the very next day for India. Clearly the divine forces were directing me to my destiny.

When I arrived at my Guru's temple in South India two days later, everyone said, "We were expecting you today. Swamy told us you were coming. He's been waiting." Swamy welcomed me with his usual boyish grin. He was as overjoyed to see me as I was to see him. A deep silence played between us as our mutual love and affection filled the space and vibrated around us. The atmosphere was charged with the spiritual sanctity of the moment, much like when the long-lost son returns home. Words can't describe the fullness of that silent moment. I recall that it took some effort to focus when Nagananda finally spoke. He repeated himself two or three times in broken English, telling me that he'd been sending me telepathic signals to come to India for over a year.

As I heard his voice, all I wanted to do was touch his feet. And I did. In India, touching the feet of the master symbolizes acknowledgment of a transcendental experience beyond mind and body, in that worldless and wordless, timeless realm of pure spirit.

I had been receiving Swamy's telepathic signals, but must admit that I chose to ignore them and focus on my career and the demands of the material world; in other words—on my ego. Telepathic and spiritual signals can be subtle. Society conditions us to listen exclusively to the voice of reason and seeming practicality. How often have you received spiritual guidance, only to turn away from it? Have you ever received a strong hunch that you failed to act upon? The spiritual masters often communicate with one by creating an impression about what should be done. Whether the recipient heeds such a signal is another matter entirely. From youth on, we receive no encouragement to listen to the inner promptings.

Western society rewards engineers, computer programmers, doctors, lawyers and scientists. These individuals are the "Gurus" of the West. The poets, artists, dancers, musicians and yogis are not rewarded. To be a poet you must be somewhat insane. You must be willing to venture away from the herd to uncover your own truth. Society tends to view this as madness. Creativity is usually valued after the mastery stage. Picasso is honored and rewarded now, but this does not mean that young, struggling artists who may have Picasso's potential are encouraged. We give them sound advice; "Get a real job." Society needs to recognize the important contribution that sensitive individuals make. It is this sensitivity that enriches culture.

Many people are unhappy because they embrace careers in which they cannot devote themselves to their soul's passion. Dutifully, they slave away in corporate bureaucracy when their entire being yearns to create pottery or sculpture; to farm or garden, or teach; to paint or play music, or write; to dance or do yoga, or cook. Some follow the more accepted paths just to win their parents' approval. Others bury their vision because there is very little financial support in society for the creative impulse.

My own struggle with this lack of support for discovering the inner self had cost me a fortune. I worked at being a teacher, a massage therapist, a soldier, a chiropractor—always with the goal to save enough of my wages to make it to India to receive the instruction for which my soul constantly thirsted. There was little recognition in my peer group for the powerful urge I always felt to further my spiritual dimension. In this, I was as much an outcast as the struggling dancer, artist or poet.

After I was with Swamy Nagananda for several days, he instructed me, "Go away now and travel. Do not stay anywhere for more than forty-eight hours. Come back on December 25, and I will initiate you into the Swamy Order."

My first feeling was "Finally! Yes, that makes sense! Of course!" After all the years of spiritual devotion I'd invested, this seemed to be the most logical conclusion. I knew at that moment I was in Swamy "wonderland" and I was prepared for the impossible to happen at any turn.

The practice of ceaseless travel would connect me to an ancient Indian spiritual tradition of nonviolence, known as Jainism. The Jain monks follow this rule of moving every forty-eight hours for life. Swamy was reminding me of the principle of tapasya, which is sacrifice in order to reap a spiritual reward, while putting me in touch with the roots of nonviolence; a guiding principle of *prema*.

I left my Guru's temple with pangs of loneliness. There is always the possibility when you leave the master that you'll never again see him on the physical plane. And I also began to have mixed feelings, a sense of trepidation that I was about to become a Swamy. When Buddha was facing enlightenment, the whole kingdom of *Mara*, or evil, rose up to prevent his flowering. I had no idea what lay before me in the month prior to my initiation. But I knew I would somehow be going through a type of death, and God would create whatever situation was required to make me ready. I knew that my ego would have to die for the re-birth to take place.

I departed from the temple, riding with Babu, the taxi driver who had brought me on the difficult six-hour trip to Sri Sri Swamy Nagananda's ashram from the Windsor Manor Hotel in Bangalore. As we drove away, my eyes came to rest on the statue of Krishna mounted on the dashboard of Babu's car. Krishna was an *avatar*—a living representative of God like Jesus, Buddha or Babaji. He is portrayed as a dancing flute-bearing deity with brilliant blue skin. Krishna devotees are much more common among North Indian seekers, and we were in the South. This was intriguing to me, and I asked Babu about his Krishna statue. Babu's limited command of English caused him to assume from my question that I was a Krishna follower, and he immediately wanted to take me to a Krishna temple. At this moment, Krishna was not the focus of my journey to India! Nonetheless, I didn't want to offend Babu, so I held my tongue. It would have been futile to object in any case. Once a devout Hindu has the opportunity to visit a temple, nothing gets them to veer off course. I admire this, but it can be maddening when you're the passenger in a taxi in India. A driver can instantly lose command of the English language if it will accomplish the goal of getting you to the temple. Babu was taking us to a Krishna temple—no ifs, ands or buts.

Americans have had little exposure to Krishna. Most people probably think of Hare Krishnas asking for donations at the airport. This would be comparable to a Hindu whose sense of Christianity came solely from fundamentalist preachers on television. The Hare Krishnas may be on a path to God, but theirs is not the only way to approach Krishna.

Hinduism, in general, is little understood by Westerners. If you ask the average Christian about Hindus, they would say, "They worship idols of stone and wood." In fact, a similar simplistic reduction could be used by a Hindu to describe a Christian: "Christians pray to a stone, bronze or wood statue of a man nailed to a cross." Both Christians and Hindus use symbols as tools to focus their prayers. Hinduism is a religion that has stood the test of time for thousands of years—far longer than Christianity. Most of the major world religions took birth from Hinduism, or were strongly influenced by it. Hinduism is a supremely tolerant path that recognizes and accepts that God has many forms and names. Hindus regard all spiritual paths as valid as long as they don't call for the destruction of another path. This is not to say Hindus have never gone to war in the name of religion—most traditions have had experience with this failure, which is not the fault of the religions, but rather of practitioners who lose sight of the teachings themselves.

I once visited a famous Catholic church on the beach in Madras, India, which contained the remains of the apostle Saint Thomas. The Hindus have hidden statues of their elephant god Ganesha, in quiet corners of the church. In paintings and statuary, faces of Jesus and Mary are dotted with red and yellow *kumkum* on their foreheads, while garlands of flowers adorn their shoulders in the traditional Hindu way. Of course, the Hindu accepts Jesus as a savior. Hinduism has had many saviors, and these saviors have also performed astounding miracles. Some of the miracles make the turning of water into wine seem a modest accomplishment.

Hindus believe Jesus is a Son of God and will be happy to tell you about another Son of God—Buddha. Talk to them about the Virgin Mary and they will discuss a litany of female saints: Mother Theresa, Kali, Durga, Radha, Sita, Ananda Mayi Ma, Ammachi, etc. Yes, they include Mother Theresa as one of the divine beings who worked in the sacred land of India.

Hindus don't accept the idea that Jesus is the *only* way to God. They also can't understand the Islamic attitude that if you kill an infidel you are assured a place in Heaven. No, the Hindu wants only to honor all religions and to let all individuals be on the path that works best for them. From the Hindu point of view, just as all rivers flow to the ocean, all religions flow toward God. Christians who attempt to convert Hindus usually have a difficult time.

Hinduism is full of stories of various Gurus who have brought the dead back to life. In modern times, the *avatar* Sathya Sai Baba has brought two people—medically certified as dead—back to life. The Yogis understand the principle of the life force and how to restore it to a body. The science of yoga has examined the sacred magnetic energies of life more than 10,000 years. Hinduism is the major religion of the land of India. Yoga is a system of self-exploration, which is independent of any religious tradition. However, since yoga took birth in India, many Yogis were born Hindus. They honor their religious roots, but the practice of yoga can exist within any religion. Not all Hindus do yoga, and—for that matter—not all Indians are Hindu. India is a melting pot of religions—even more so than the United States.

The science of yoga coalesced in the sixth century in the writings of the brilliant sage Pantanjali, who before he wrote the *Yoga Sutras*, had already developed Ayurvedic medicine, the traditional healing system that has thrived since ancient times in India. It is believed that Babaji initiated Pantanjali into yoga.

Babu enthused to me in broken Indian-English about the Krishna temple we were heading toward.

"It is only two hours, sir," he affirmed in clipped Indian English, "We'll go straight away. Maybe we'll stop for some coffee."

Babu knew I didn't drink coffee, but he loved to stop and bring me some in a cup of dubious cleanliness.

"Is it far?" I persisted in asking.

"Not far, not far," he answered. "Only one, two hours, sir."

I was in India with nothing but openness to God, and I knew the spiritual masters would direct me to those places that would bring me the information I needed to further my spiritual mission. I was abiding in the mental space of gently accepting all as God's grace, and knowing that life is being divinely directed. From this perspective I quietly acquiesced to the trip.

Having used the primitive restroom facilities at the earlier ashram and taken some water, I was prepared for the two-hour journey ahead. The cab didn't have air conditioning—not unusual in India—so the inside was hot and dusty. We needed some air, but only the driver's window was down because we were traveling over unpaved dirt roads. Clouds of dry orange Indian clay billowed into the cab with each mile, and I would often find myself choking or coughing up dirt. I could feel the dirt on my teeth and gums.

"Master, do you like *bhajans*?" Babu asked. *Bhajans* are the beautiful spiritual songs of the Indian people.

"Yes," I replied. Babu grinned, showing a mouth full of healthy white teeth, which is common with India's vegetarian population. He was no doubt happy to play some music for the drive ahead, as he opened his glove box and revealed several cassette tapes featuring devotional Hindu music. The tape player was soon filling our car with the faraway lilting sound of male and female devotees singing to Krishna. This is a unique sound heard in and around the temples throughout India.

Most of India still remains on a different clock from the rest of the world. When an Indian says, "No problem sir, the restroom is coming soon," this means, "Sometime within the next seventy-two hours we will locate a Western-style toilet." The same can be true for a request for bottled water or food. They have sensitivity to the Western traveler there. They know that we don't use the streets, or the Indian-style holes in the floor—which are surrounded by bugs and much nastier than that—but it is simply difficult in their country to accommodate our needs. Notwithstanding, they try.

Knowing this, I often fasted while traveling, and had conditioned myself to get by on only a few sips of water during the day, saving my thirst for the hotel at night where I could drink my fill and have restroom access. Despite the heat and my cotton-mouthed dehydration, I never drank more than one or two sips at any given time, to prevent my bladder from getting too full. I was frustrated by this aspect of travel in India, because I knew from my studies that the body needs as much as sixteen glasses of liquid a day. This was the so-called "winter" season of South India—the hot, dry time without the cooling monsoons—and the sun was blazing unmercifully. Fortunately, I had learned the Yogic technique of concentrating on the suprasternal notch—the U-shaped groove at the base of the neck—to reduce these symptoms.

Long meditations were a necessity, and I craved them. I had traveled all this way to go within, and whether I was in a cab or not, I knew that what was going to transpire spiritually would take place inwardly. My sitting lotus style and barefoot in the back seat of Babu's cab seemed to give him a sense of pride. He approved of the fact that I was meditating. Almost as soon as I settled into the position, I opened the burlap shoulder bag I'd purchased in Bangalore and pulled from it the memo pad on which my beautiful wife Marilyn had written her farewell note to me in Los Angeles. With an eager longing, I held it reverently and tenderly in my hand, exhaled out and took a deep breath, which I held and then slowly exhaled while connecting to her. I knew that time and space could never diminish our love for each other. Touching the pad, I felt myself touching the sweet face of my darling. Then I slowly opened my eyes, moist with tears, and—for the umpteenth time—I read her written expressions of love to me—anguishing at the physical separation.

> *My dearest, my darling Don . . .*
>
> *As you read this, know that—far away—every beat of my heart is for you. I'm never without you. I carry you in every cell of my being. I am one with you, I breathe in you, I see in you, I hear in you, I sleep and dream in you.*
>
> *And if God blesses me, all my dreams are of you, my Don.*
>
> *You have touched my heart like no other; you are my heart. Until you return to me, I will live for you.*
>
> *I am yours forever.*
>
> *Marilyn*

Marilyn is a well-known person—the co-author of the book *Fit For Life*, and several other health- and food-related books she's written on her own. We met in 1992, and from the moment I saw her, I knew she was my soul mate. No words were exchanged, but I recognized her from my dreams. We were both on the threshold of messy divorces and hurting deeply from relationships that had failed. The moment I saw her, I said to myself, "What's happened to my sunflower?" Sunflowers for me were symbolic of God's awesome creative force. In the six years since we met, we'd never been apart.

No words can ever capture the perfect love expressed partly through the spiritual, mental, emotional, physical and sexual rapture between Marilyn and me. I say "partly" because our love is so much greater than any one element—and even more than the sum of all the parts. It's completeness itself. Encompassed within my love for Marilyn, was my love of her three children. I consider them my own children.

As I held her letter and cried, I dropped into a deep meditative state. I often saw Marilyn with my meditative vision and telepathically sent her my love and *shakti.* In my meditation, I saw her as a core of divine energy that was radiating love into the world. At that point, I was sensing her flowering as a spiritual teacher of love in tandem with the tapasya I was undergoing in India. I could feel that the Eastern wisdom that was birthing in me was being complemented by the birth taking place within her in the West. As wonderful as my meditations were, none compared to the richness of being in her presence.

Beau, Marilyn's eighteen-year-old son, frequently entered my meditations. He was crying out for a rewarding life. His soul was demanding relevant work and companionship with others. It seemed that his ego, mind and body were imprisoned within a castle of some dark, sticky material. No matter what he would try to do, his vision could not be launched as it was trapped within the stickiness. Whatever this castle was, Beau needed to get out of it. Against the strong yearnings of his soul for spiritual nourishment, the darkness wanted Beau to be trapped in materialism.

Marilyn's twenty-eight-year-old daughter, Lisa, appeared to me almost daily. She was hungry for spiritual vibrations and was yearning to find her life companion. When I saw her counseling others spiritually—working with people unknown to me—then I would see her happy. The unique aspect of her contact with me was a field of color that surrounded her, and reached out toward others.

Greg, Marilyn's thirty-year-old son, also appeared regularly. Greg was opening his heart and desired to go more deeply into his spiritual nature. He was drawing healing vibrations from me.

There were others, sometimes thousands of faces, that would flood into my conscious vision. To all I would send vibrations of love, health and happiness.

After the visits to soul friends, my meditation settled into a quiet thought-free state of blissful silence. Many times, I would be jarred out of my tranquility by the blaring of a horn as a bus or a huge commercial truck careened past our taxi, a hair-width from disaster. My ability to stay in a deep, unaffected state increased with such intense practice! In India, I came to see these frequent encounters as God's way of testing the depth of my meditative state.

In India, travel by automobile is highly risky. Fatal collisions are a daily occurrence. Ninety-nine percent of the cars lack seat belts. Most of the cars are twenty to thirty years old with bad brakes and treadless tires. If you should get into a serious accident, you can forget about an ambulance coming. There are no ambulances! To make matters worse, hospital facilities may be several days' distance away. Even if you do make it to a hospital, it will be one that is most likely primitive.

The reality is brutal. Forget anesthetics and antibiotics. The staff suffers from a language barrier, and there is no guarantee they will admit you without insurance. In most cases, American medical insurance is worthless anyway. Many tourists who are involved in accidents finally make it to a hospital only to find they've been robbed of both passport and wallet.

Babu's sincere affirmations of "one or two hours" notwithstanding, it was more than six hours later when we reached our destination. My sole intent upon arriving was to immediately race to a restroom, then locate some potable water. We were in a remote area—about ten kilometers beyond the last small village we had passed—and I wasn't comfortable relieving myself in the streets Indian-style. There are people everywhere in India. I hoped there would be some privacy at the temple for this ordinary need. If there wasn't, I intended to return to the village immediately.

The temple was on a hill overlooking a valley, inside a compound about the size of a football field. A solid white wall about two meters high surrounded it. I estimated it to be at least a few centuries old—and it was unscrubbed. Babu stopped in front of a large iron gate that was blocked by a guard in a white *lungi*—the diaper-like wrap worn around the hips by Indian men in the countryside. Babu and the man spoke excitedly. Apparently a highly evolved spiritual master called "Babaji" had arrived hours before and was in residence. No one in the distant village knew of his arrival, and thus there were present only about a dozen of his closest disciples—who had arrived with him. Babaji is a common name given to many Gurus. While I was happy to hear a master was nearby, I was in no way connecting the name "Babaji" to *the* Babaji, the immortal Yogi-Christ of India to whom I had prayed when I was a child.

I had visited the ashrams of numerous well-known modern Gurus, and they were always found in *new* ashrams. This rustic, out-of-the-way, run-down location led me to assume that this could not *possibly* be a "famous" or recognized teacher. If he were important there would have been crowds of American, Japanese, Russian, Australian and European seekers clogging the area. I was focusing on getting to a restroom—and feeling somewhat despondent because this temple looked too rustic and unused to have any clean facilities. My parched throat was crying out for some fresh, pure water.

I was in despair of finding any relief at this rustic temple. I feared the village I'd thought to rely on would also prove useless for my needs. I began to calculate how long it would take to reach the nearest modern city. I told myself I could stay here for fifteen or twenty minutes at most—long enough not to be rude. Then we would travel immediately back to Bangalore. My heart sank with the realization that Bangalore was a good ten to twelve hours away! How had I allowed myself to be passively dragged into this whole episode by Babu? I briefly considered that he had perhaps initiated this journey simply to earn more money with a ridiculously long taxi ride.

My sour mental state notwithstanding, it felt good to be putting on my Birkenstock sandals, knowing that I could step out of the car and give my leg muscles a rest. After hours of being cramped in the car, I ambled stiffly over to the gate. I noticed in the distance that a young man in a white robe was standing on the steps of the temple, waving to me as if to an old friend. He motioned for me to come in through the gate. About a dozen Indian men stood and sat near him at the entrance to the temple. I waved back—not knowing whom I was waving to—and turned back to the car to get the book that I had co-authored with Marilyn. I usually kept it with me to identify myself in new situations. Along with the book, I grabbed my sport pack containing my wallet, passport and money. I trusted Babu, but I'd learned from experience that thieves might approach the car while I was out of sight within the temple.

When I came back to the gate and went through, I saw that the friendly man in the white robe had moved from the doorway of the temple, and was now about sixty yards away under the large banyan tree across the compound. The same men were still around him, but he was now sitting in a *jhula*, a bamboo chair, that doubled as a swing. I was surprised that he and his group had moved so far and settled under the tree so quickly, and so quietly! It had taken me less than a minute to go to the cab. It also occurred to me that I saw no vehicle that could have brought Babaji and his entourage to this remote outpost. The only vehicle in sight was Babu's Ambassador cab.

The temple was on top of a mesa that looked out over miles of lush tropical landscape. There were no nearby rivers, which probably explained the apparent lack of activity at the temple compound. It was too far removed from any population to receive any kind of traffic. It also didn't have the amenities of the famous Indian temples—no food stands or places to put your sandals, no film vendors—not even professional beggars.

I could feel waves of spiritual vibrations coming from the young man in white. It was as if he were a fountain sending forth streams of spiritual nourishment to the surrounding area. Even the usual cackling crows and chittering monkeys were quiet. I approached slowly, as if being pulled by a conveyor belt. I wasn't aware of walking. My muscles somehow found the ability to move on their own. Our eyes connected with a oneness, and what I'm relating here was taking place through this shared vision. I was seeing him see me as he was seeing me see him. It was like an infinite mirrored image—a mirror bouncing off a mirror bouncing off a mirror. My body took on the quiet demeanor of sleep. There was no longer the impatient need for water, nor was my body signaling the urgent need of a restroom. There was a transcendental reality—somewhat like sleep—that was beyond the physical body and mind and the perception of what was taking place. This isn't as strange as it sounds. It is typical to be unaware of bodily demands during deep sleep. We even lose awareness of the pain of a terrible toothache when we fall into a state of peaceful sleep, where there are no difficulties.

I was experiencing the Hindu teaching of *Maya*—the world as illusion—a projection from the mind. Just as a spider spins a web from itself, this world is spun from our ego and mind. Nothing else existed but this moment and those incredible eyes. I bowed reverently at the feet of this mysterious master and sat in a cross-legged position in front of him.

Silently, I handed the *Fitonics* book to him. His slender, graceful hand reached forth to take it.

"Thank you, Swamiji," he said. Those were the first words he uttered to me, and they sent me reeling.

Only seven hours earlier, my Guru had informed me I had been called to India to become a Swamy. Now, for the second time that day, I was hearing that title. I was not in a region of the world where phones, faxes and pagers exist. This temple didn't even have electricity! There were no phones or electrical lines anywhere in sight. Swamy Nagananda could not have called to announce my arrival. Here was a synchronicity I couldn't fathom.

The white-robed figure before me who had absorbed me into his state of radiance was calling me a Swamy, and yet I was not wearing Swamy clothing, and my ceremony with Sri Sri Swamy Nagananda was still several weeks away. I hadn't even fully digested what it meant to be a Swamy, and needed to "think" about it. My mind was trying to process the idea, and it couldn't.

He seemed very pleased with the book. He spent a long time looking at the picture of Marilyn. He made several fluid yogic hand gestures or *mudras* that I knew to be a way of communicating spiritual blessings. I had involuntarily started to make these same gestures with my own hands ten years earlier. He looked off into the distance, and I sensed he was strengthening some inner connection to Marilyn.

"Your wife is very powerful Yogi. She will bring happiness to millions. Acha! Tch!" He closed his eyes and grew silent.

I suddenly knew in a dizzying flash that I was in the presence of Babaji. The body before me was clearly no more than twenty-four-years of physical age. He was a light-skinned Indian, and I noticed again his long, slender hands. Of course! He was wearing the white robe of the perfected spiritual adept. The men around him were deep in meditation and were doing a form of breathing meditation I knew to be Babaji's special technique. A few of the devotees were adding wood to a fire. There was no need for warmth. I didn't know why they were doing it.

"This book has much good information," he said, "but you are a Swamy and this is not totally Swamy's message. The West needs a Swamy. Krishna has brought you to me." I remembered reading in Paramhansa Yogananda's autobiography that Krishna had initiated Babaji. His mission was to carry forth the path of Yoga and to see that the sacred and secret steps to spiritual meditation were not lost in the modern era.

"A new time is with us," Babaji said, his eyes holding mine. "Many political forces are shaping world. China will try to snuff out spiritual flame. In time China may invade India and other countries. It is only by creating many powerful spiritual leaders and spiritual vibrations of peace that this wave can be stopped. The Americas and Europe are ready for a Western Swamy. There are many there who thirst for experience of God within. Show them how to reach God and fill them with natural peace and spiritual vibrations. You and your wife will bring the message of *Prema*—divine love—to all people who desire to receive the grace of the *Avatars*. Together you will reach many hungry souls who wish only to be more God conscious. You will find that young in your country are ready; what they call "X" generation." Babaji chuckled sweetly at that label.

"The X is powerful spiritual symbol, it contains both Hindu swastika[2] and Christian cross. This generation must be taught power of the cross. The cross is not just sacred symbol for Christians. It has significant Egyptian roots. This generation knows you cannot name God, so they call themselves X generation. They are not lost generation. They are ones who will find God within. They are "found" generation. They sense what is wrong with materialistic life, and they yearn for more. This generation is ready to embrace spiritual life and assist you in bringing peace into new era. This generation must not make mistake of last century. I sent many spiritual leaders during late 1800s to America. Instead of turning within, Americans became seduced by promises of science for more material prosperity."

"Babaji, Marilyn has some children in this generation." I assumed he knew this, but said it as if I were telling him something he didn't know. His hands sent forth a volley of benediction at the mention of Marilyn's name. "Lisa, Greg and..."

"Beau," he supplied, showing me his omniscience. It was not a pompous display; he was merely conversing with me as a close family member who already knew the details. I felt like I was in a tunnel, and he was a loudspeaker—even though his voice was soft. The words were being scorched into my consciousness. But words—although sincere—were like a social convention, a formality. Everything that was happening was way beyond the words. There was a mystical transmission connected to light—like fireworks exploding against a dark sky. Simultaneously, I felt like a desert plant soaking up the rain during a monsoon. Still, there was a timeless quality and a greater reality in his presence that made the ordinary physical plane seem like a stage set. I felt that we were all the hired actors and actresses of God's movie. Nothing in the physical world seemed substantial. I closed my eyes and opened them, and it made no difference. The spiritual dimension was so strong that if I never ate, never moved again, it wouldn't matter.

I felt a complete oneness, a holiness so profound that peace and joy followed it like the shadow follows the body. His voice again beckoned to my mind to attend to his words, and the words were like art. I didn't feel the need to look at him. The shared inner reality transcended his physical presence. The physical presence was just more *Maya*, and I knew I didn't need to look at the *Maya*. What was real was the inner world I was sharing with him. It was what I am in my essence—what we *all* are.

"Beau needs to slow down," Babaji continued. "He is going too fast in some areas of his life. He will awaken," he said. "Tch!"

I knew Beau to be strong and extremely independent. Inwardly, I knew he was already way ahead of many of his peers.

"Can you bless Greg?" I asked. Again, I knew that Babaji was already doing this, and yet my soul wanted to personally make the request. I wanted to be absolutely sure he helped my oldest son. He bobbed his head Indian-fashion.

"Living in California, is it?" he asked with an omniscient smile. "Tch. Babaji will take care. The karmas are working out for him, and he knows this. Greg also must live the spiritual life. Greg is friend to all and he will now become friend to Greg."

When I asked him about Greg, I had opened my eyes to look at him. Now I found it awkward to continue to stare into those deep brown pools called "eyes." It felt improper. I looked down.

"Lisa?" he asked softly. He was waiting for me to say something, and yet I felt I should wait for him to tell me. I took a deep breath and waited for a few long seconds. Babaji took the decision from me.

"Lisa is advanced soul who has been mistreated. There was a bad man in her life. She struggles to know why. She wants to go forward. Lisa seeks not to escape life through yoga, but to embrace hunger for God. She must meditate more. When she turns fully to spiritual life, she will be happy. Baba will bless her. Baba protects Lisa in many ways. Baba brings Lisa many blessings."

The way he said Lisa's name, it was a caress, and clearly he knew Lisa as a being of incredible beauty. There was a tone to the way he said her name I will never forget.

"Baba," I said softly, "you said 'bad man.'"

"Yes, there are bad men. Always remember, there are good apples and bad apples. There are two principles to the creation of this plane. It is principle of Good that creates goodness, and principle of Evil that creates evil. This is the way it is on this planet."

His statement had a profound significance for me. From my prior perspective, there were only good souls who sometimes behaved badly. I wanted more of an explanation.

"Bad man?" I repeated.

"Yes, bad. So much filth covers natural goodness. One cannot cover filth with positive thinking. One must first atone for actions and go through purification. If they do nothing, Mother Karma will reform."

His answer seemed to contain both a Catholic and Hindu explanation. Babaji was saying that it was important for one who has sinned to acknowledge the sin, seek purification, and atone for the sin.

"You mean bad men *can* change?" I asked.

"Of course. The good is always working to reform the bad," he said softly.

"There are other bad men," Babaji continued. "They come to India and want to learn shortcuts to spiritual powers. Their intent is to return to America and display these powers to others. They teach motivation, psychology and firewalking. Their goal is profit-centered. These people not trying to bring others to God consciousness. Their lives are about acquiring personal power in an attempt to strengthen their egos. Beware of wolves in sheep's clothing. They parade their learning with arrogance and pomposity. There is no humility. These are not Yogis; they are Bhogis. They will take nothing from this country, nothing. Their cups already full with the importance of their egos. Spirituality can never be reduced to television commercials and DCs!"

"DCs?"

"Tapes!"

"Oh, you mean CDs," I said. "What was that word, *Bhogi*?"

"Pleasure seekers! These people just want to indulge their senses. They tell others to follow their example. Find a mate, have lots of sex, make lots of money, and this is meaning of success. These charlatans and their representatives come to this sacred country, trying to find shortcuts to God. They throw American dollars around, in belief spirituality can be purchased like common item. Never was true saint produced through shortcut. The tragedy is they lead people to look for easy way. One must have discipline and be consistent. Real happiness is earned from spiritual work. It is reward that comes from right effort consistently applied."

"Does Marilyn like to sing?" Babaji sang, changing the subject. He didn't say her name; he "sang" it.

"Yes," I said. He laughed sweetly and some of the men around him laughed at his laugh.

"Singing will be good for Western people. Marilyn senses this in her heart. She is a natural *Bhakti.*" He again nodded his head; then he lifted his hand and wrote in the air. This is a method used to send blessings.

His face took on a serious look.

"You will not see your mother again in this lifetime. When she dies she will come to me and know better life in her next incarnation. It was I who took her from you at early age, so that you would turn toward God. You must now begin to see divine mother in all women."

His words struck me hard. They took my breath away. My mother had left me when I was just a toddler, and I only reconnected to her in my mid-twenties. For many reasons, I had been unable to see my mother during the last few years. The realization that I wouldn't see her again was painful, yet, in Babaji's presence I felt the divine guidance behind all of life and could therefore accept it as divine will.

I saw that my yearning for God as a young child was definitely the result of my mother's departure—Babaji's "blessing." I always sought my mother's love in the form of prayer and devotion toward God, but the feelings were incomplete. So, I turned to meditation to find the yoga—or union—with my Beloved. Earthly parents do their best, but they do not have the power of our cosmic parents. The Hindu tradition is replete with couples serving as divine mothers and fathers. As a whole, the Christian tradition tended to focus solely on Jesus, the male figure, while ignoring Mary Magdalene,[3] the female. This tends to bring a one-sided development to one's spiritual growth.

"It is your *dharma* to bring new spirituality to new era. Teach Western hemisphere about divine love. Teach meditation for rejuvenation of its followers. Meditation will bring real peace to planet because it will not be words, but rather true experience of peaceful divinity that blossoms in the practitioners. The young in body and the young at heart want to experience God. When we think old then God is far away. I will send to you the sweet people."

I looked at his own youthful, peaceful face and knew the truth of his words. "No form of politics can ever eradicate this spiritual peace," he added, looking back at me with subtle reference to the Chinese invasion he'd spoken about earlier. "The whole world will rise up against you, but I will be for you and that is enough."

"Are you going to teach me your meditation?" I asked.

"Tch," he nodded his assent, Indian-fashion with that unique side-to-side bobbing of the head and hand gesture, indicating that my request had already been answered affirmatively.

"I will teach you some. The rest you will uncover in *Premananda*—land of meditation. I will meet you there from time to time to give you what you need."

I was familiar with this process thanks to Sri Sri Swamy Nagananda. He had the power to enter my dreams and to teach me. If only some of my college classes could have been absorbed in this way! I wished at that moment that I could be in the presence of both Sri Sri Swamy Nagananda and Babaji.

Swamy Nagananda was my first Guru. He began to enter my dreams and my meditations when I was seven years old. When I saw him as a child, he would wave his hand and materialize pink and blue candy out of thin air. I didn't know then what this miracle was called, but I understood it was a blessing. When I accepted the candy in my dreams, I would be overcome with bliss, and I would anticipate my next meditation with great longing. Swamy's presence in my life made it difficult for me to be away from meditation for very long. I *always* yearned to be meditating. My outer world was dwarfed by the inner world.

At night, when my family slept, I would sit cross-legged in my bunk, meditating for hours. I was only a little kid, and I already had a strong relationship with my Guru. But I didn't know his name.

I began searching in the outer world for Swamy Nagananda in 1978, when I was twenty-three. I made numerous trips to India, but it wasn't until 1984 that I finally found him. I had spent that summer at the huge ashram of Sathya Sai Baba in Puttaparthi, sitting eight or more hours a day in blazing tropical sun on the hard-baked earth, meditating and waiting for a five-minute glimpse of the Indian *avatar*. There were twenty or thirty thousand people always there, clamoring for some small favor from the master. His acknowledgments came with the rarity of a winning lottery ticket—seemingly random and impossible to find.

One day, I couldn't contain my yearning any longer. I wrote a letter to Sai Baba, and spent an extra two hours in the scorching sun to be sure I'd sit in the front row when he walked that afternoon through the temple courtyard. The crowds around me that day seemed larger and more oppressive than ever. As the *avatar* approached, I held out my letter, praying with all my might that he might stoop to take it from my hand. It contained my heartfelt request that Sai Baba send me to a more personal teacher. At that moment in my life that was all I wanted.

As Sai Baba approached, I could feel his intense vibrations. "*Please* take my letter," was the prayer I kept repeating. My eyes were closed. I couldn't bear to watch him pass me. Then I felt the gentle tug on my letter, and I opened my eyes just in time to see him turn away.

The next day, I took a taxi to a temple I'd heard about from a Catholic Indian driver by the name of Francis. It was a small temple, humble, nestled in the bug-infested jungle, and by comparison to Puttaparthi, one could hardly feel anything of significance could go on there. As I removed my shoes at the temple door, I saw a young Swamy my age with a handsome face sitting on a lone chair in the semidarkness. He beckoned for me to come near, and as I sat at his feet, he offered to read my palm.

"How disappointing," I thought, "and how mundane." Palm readers in India are as common as hot dog vendors in New York. I acquiesced to avoid hurting the Swamy's feelings, and he proceeded to tell me about my future. I listened half-heartedly, yearning to be on a plane back to the United States. In my mind I savored the image of an ice-cold Coca-Cola waiting for me at the airport in Los Angeles. I was burned-out on India; my search, the endless rice and curry, and the hot soda pop I was always drinking because the water was unsafe.

When the Swamy finished, I made my polite excuses and left the temple through a side door to look for my taxi. The moment I stepped out into that shaded courtyard, my skin felt the shivers of the soul's recognition. *I knew that place.* I'd been there hundreds of times in my dreams and meditations. I was standing on the exact spot I would always visit when the Guru of my childhood and I were together. At that moment, my palm-reading Swamy appeared from the temple door. I spun around to face him.

"I know who you are!" I exclaimed. "When I was a boy, you used to come to me in my dreams and meditations. I would be sitting on this spot and you would make pink and blue candy come from out of the air. And you'd give it to me and then I would have the best meditations."

"Yes, yes," the Swamy said, bobbing his head in the characteristic Indian waggle, waving his hand in a circular motion and materializing a large purple candy that he popped directly into my mouth.

I tasted the familiar sweetness of my childhood dreams. Sathya Sai Baba had answered my prayer. I found my Guru.

Thirteen years later, as Babaji and I stood facing one another, a strong breeze popped out of nowhere, rustled through the magnificent tree above, and embraced us. I perceived that this wasn't an ordinary breeze, but the element of air at Babaji's service. In Hindu mythology the wind is the domain of Hanuman, the monkey God who served the great *avatar* Ram. The wind symbolizes *prana*—the vital and divine essence of all life. Hanuman is symbolic of undivided service to God's mission.

I recalled the many times I'd spent in the desert with my father, during the time of my youth when I was meditating on Babaji. My father—who's half Native American—told me then that the sudden pop of wind is a divine communication that Native Americans know to welcome and embrace. That kind of wind is a messenger. I learned to look around and pay attention whenever I felt it. As the wind arrived at this moment, simultaneously the crows and monkeys who had been silent came to life, as if they were in touch with this elemental force as well.

"*Vayu*,"[4] said Babaji, leaning forward and placing his palm upon my head. Just as mysteriously, the crows and monkeys were hushed once again.

"Close your eyes and see me within," he urged. Inwardly, with my eyes closed, I could see him sitting in the swing, smiling. My inner vision was as strong as my outer vision. I saw him so clearly it was as if I didn't have eyelids or was seeing him with x-ray eyes. Behind him I could see a tear-drop-shaped blue light coming in. I was transfixed by it—mesmerized. It was as large as his body and moving toward him. As I watched it, it wasn't expanding and contracting. Yet it was simultaneously thumb-size and human-size. I couldn't understand; this was a mind-snap.

The light began to communicate to me. In a transcendental knowing—a perception rather than a reasoning—I saw the changing of shape as the playfulness of God symbolized by Krishna. This playfulness is referred to as *leela*—the divine play of God to win our attention and our hearts. None of the words on this page can capture even a fraction of the glory of that revelation. At that moment, the light provided me with the understanding that it was the body of Krishna—the blue one. I wasn't sitting there reasoning this out—it was simply communicated to me.

I had the sudden insight that Krishna had played an important role in my life. Gently had he played his flute, creating the music to guide me. I suddenly had another insight. *Life is music*! As the Bible says, in the beginning was the word—*sound*. The Universe is music—*everything* is music. The fundamental movement of life itself is rhythmic and musical. That's why the Hindus, the Native Americans, and practically all traditions dance and sing and move in their love of God. God is music. That's why the singing of chants and hymns brings us closer to God.

Life is rich with sound and life *is* sound. It's music. The yogis have a name for it. They call the celestial sounds of life *nadam*, and we begin to hear this sweet music in meditation. The scientists think creation is matter and energy, but it's more than that. It's the vibration of music—*the Song of God*. That's what "Bhagavad Gita"[5] means—the Song of God. The revelation of the blue light continued. Life isn't only music. It's color, it's poetry. God is an artist—a musician—a *Creator*. Artists, poets, dancers, and musicians . . . *rejoice*! The more creative we become, the closer we come to our Creator.

When Krishna plays his flute, it creates a "breeze" of *prana*, or spiritual energy, that an attuned devotee may feel in various forms such as goose bumps, or hot or cold flashes running through the body. The flute is the *shushumna*—the center of the spiritual spine in your body. The holes are the seven *chakras*[6]—our whirling spiritual energy centers.

My first encounter with the blue light, or *rupam*, as it is known in Sanskrit, happened in childhood. Many times I would sit to meditate, and I would see a blue dot in the center of my forehead—the location of the third eye. This blue dot would vary in appearance, but was similar to the after-image of a camera flash. It was from this blue dot that my beloved Swamy Nagananda would appear to me. I didn't know who he was, and wouldn't find him in India for almost a quarter of a century, but the *darshans*—the visions I had of my Guru—were sweet. In fact, I thrived on them. Whenever I sat for meditation I would look for this blue light, because I knew from experience that wonderful visions and insights would manifest in this light. The blue light was my friend. In the way that children enjoy "imaginary playmates" I enjoyed the comforting aspect of my blue light. On some occasions, other colors would appear. All colors are spiritual and each has its own dimension, its own value.

A *Siddha* Guru is one who is fully realized. The word *siddha* means "cooked," which in this sense indicates that such a being has worked off all negative karmas and is purified adequately to live in the "blue realm." The *Siddha* Guru, Swamy Muktananda, told me in the 1970s that the blue light—which he called the "blue pearl"—is the spiritual body of the *Siddhas*. A *Siddha* is a spiritual being who lives within a physical body. *Siddhas* have continual contact with the divine realms through the blue light, and are highly regarded by Hindus because of their powerful abilities to bring blessings. Their greatest blessing is to offer others the *experience* of God. The blue light is one of the great mysteries of spiritual life. It is very tiny and yet it contains an entire spiritual universe. It is the realm of consciousness where all God-realized beings communicate with one another.

I've been teaching meditation for twenty-five years. In my weekend seminars, typically there are four meditation sessions, two each day—one in the morning and one in the afternoon. These sessions are designed to lead my participants to *prema*—the divine love buried deep within the heart, and *ananda*—the natural bliss of the soul. I take them deeper and deeper into meditation with each session. Meditation is like peeling an onion. As you go deeper and deeper into meditation you uncover more and more layers of divinity. You continually let go of any darkness that keeps you from seeing your inner light of beauty and truth. The darkness takes the form of fear, anger, jealousy, hatred, feelings of unworthiness, low self-esteem, victim thinking and the thousand and one ways that we talk ourselves into believing that we are very ordinary and nothing special.

Sadly, this lack of awareness of who we are is responsible for much of the misery that humans inflict upon other humans. When you truly know that everyone is a divine being on a path to God, how can you regard anyone with fear, loathing and hatred because they are not Christian or Jewish, Muslim or Buddhist? Why does religious preference matter? What difference does race make? Why should it matter what language someone speaks? Fundamental one-way-ism is responsible for spreading much hatred in the name of religion. If only everyone on a spiritual journey would learn to say, "This path works for me. I respect your path and will not try to turn you from your path. If you would like to know more about my path, I will happily share it with you. If you embrace it, I am happy. If you choose another path, or *no path*, I am happy to have been an instrument in your search." If every "one-way, only-way" religion adopted and practiced these steps, there would be so much more happiness and harmony among nations.

I felt a tremendous amount of heat, or *prana*, leave Babaji's hand and flow into the top of my head. Inwardly, I saw the image of him melt into a golden white light that permeated my entire body. I understood this was the light of *Brahman*, or God. The white part of the light was soothing, while the golden light carried a warm, invigorating influence, much like the sun.

My breathing was suspended. There was no fear or tension, and no breath. My consciousness felt like it was being pulled out of my body with a whirling, tornado motion. It was pleasant. Perhaps, I thought, this is what dying feels like. I could see the entire temple compound—my body, Babaji's body in the swing, bathed in this egg-shaped field of golden white light. The trees, the ground, everything—was filled with this iridescent energy. It wasn't so much that it had a radiant quality; *it was radiance itself*. The world as we know it comes from this field of brilliant light. Our minds project our world upon the light.

Babaji was smiling sweetly and swaying back and forth in the swing. Behind me, I could see my driver Babu approaching respectfully toward Babaji. And I could see our white Ambassador, outside the temple and behind the compound wall. The golden white light gave me "X-ray" vision.

Another strong breeze rustled through the tree, and many blue pearl-like lights floated into the field of golden white light like soap bubbles. The breeze was no ordinary wind, but rather a current of *prana* from the divine realms, announcing the arrival of the *Siddhas*. These divine beings—seemingly encapsulated in the blue bubbles—were summoned by the divine will of Babaji. They were approaching for his *Mahadarshan*. *Darshan*—a Sanskrit word—means a vision of the divine. *Maha* means great.

"Welcome to *Premananda*," Babaji spoke, breaking the silence of this out-of-body experience. The pressure of his hand on my head was light. I was unprepared for what happened next. Swamy Muktananda appeared.

He was a real flesh and blood being. I was stunned and startled when he swatted me with the large wand of peacock feathers he carried. I could smell the strong aroma of his *hina* oil. Here was my Siddha Guru, who had died over a decade earlier, now standing before me in the flesh. What mystery is this?! The shock took me even deeper within. He walked behind me and thumped me on the back with a stinging thunderclap of his hand. It was well known at his many ashrams during the 1970s that this was one of Muktananda's rarer and more powerful methods of transmitting the powerful *Siddha* blessings he generously brought to his many devotees. He looked up at Babaji, with a pleased "this-is-my-boy" look.

Baba Muktananda started his work with me nearly a quarter of a century earlier. I sought him out when I was nineteen. At the age of twenty-one, I was the only civilian, or "non-Swamy," allowed to run a Siddha Yoga ashram—as his ashrams were called. I was one of the youngest people to be certified as a Siddha yoga teacher. With all sincerity, I asked Muktananda to please transfer to me his *prema*, (divine love), *shakti* (divine energy), and *jnana* (divine wisdom). I asked him to make me fit as his vehicle for future generations—to bless me that I would be able to fully transmit the complete power of the *Siddha* energy he carried.

At that milestone in my life, he swatted me many times with his peacock feathers and pulled me to his lap, where he stroked my back. I asked him to bless my writings, that the divine energy would flow through them, so others could have the sublime experience and realization of God in their lives while reading my words. And he did. I was holding some sample letters I'd written, and he placed his hand upon them, eyes closed. When his young female translator took the letters from my hand, Baba yelled at her to return them to me. He swatted them with his peacock wand to complete the blessing.

Though Muktananda had left the physical plane in the early eighties, it was clearly only his body that was no longer with us. He lived in *Premananda* and was fully active, blessing his students. Now, sixteen years since I'd seen him so clearly, I cried at the vision of my beloved Swamy Muktananda. I knew I'd reached this pinnacle of experience with Babaji in my life because I'd had the good fortune of meeting this powerful *Siddha* Guru. In order to reach the sublime spiritual heights the seeker needs the assistance—the grace—of the *Siddha* Guru, who transmits the divine energy of *shakti*—or *prana.*

My back would be sore for days, and I relished that soreness, knowing the power of that slap. I could still feel the blow, as I wrote these lines months later. Muktananda was *there.* He clearly had a physical presence. He conveyed his benedictions to me through that swat of the peacock feathers and the slap. He was answering my youthful prayer that I be allowed to carry on his work—giving me the final touch I needed to bring the experience of the divine *prana* to the West.

Prana is the purifying divine fire. It is the element in foods that causes our bodies to radiate light. You can experience this by eating fruit and drinking fresh vegetable juices for a day. Look at your eyes, and you will see *prana* as the light shining back at you. *Prana* brings life to the body and light to the aura. The more *prana* you have, the stronger your aura. Someday forward-thinking doctors will treat people by making sure their diet and lifestyle is such that they are taking in the maximum amount of *prana.* When you receive *prana* during a spiritual encounter with a master, it is literally a life-saving transfusion of much-needed spiritual energy that recharges your batteries. Just as darkness flees from light, often negative conditions and situations flee from the sudden influx of *prana,* and many new and positive conditions take their place.

I felt a breeze pass over the top of my head—as if it were flowing from Babaji's hand—and it caused me to look up. I heard a noise like wind rustling through trees, and felt a churning sensation inside me. It seemed like somebody was turning something above me—as if I were a wind-up toy. Looking up, I saw Swamy Nagananda who emerged from the apex of the egg-shaped field of golden white light that encompassed the entire scene. Here was yet another doorway to this alternative reality. Swamy often made his arrival through some dramatic means as a way to help me remember what was *really* happening in this thing called life. He traveled down a web of silver cord[7]—so shiny it appeared like platinum—while sitting in the lotus position. He was suspended like a spider from the top of the egg, attached by the silver cord to his *Khanda* center[8] at one end, and to the top of the egg at the other. He levitated carefully down and flew around my body several times, wrapping it in the silver cord.

"I give you many powers from Mother Kali," he said. "People have good meditation from you. Kali will bring you many people. People come to you, any disease, any problem, Kali will heal." Kali is the feminine aspect of divinity. Spiritual powers come from the feminine principle, birthed from Mother Kali.

Swamy went on. "All people seeing you in dreams," he said. "You giving powers to them. Many people happy." He was strengthening my ability to travel in my spiritual body, so that I could meet the needs of spiritual seekers on the meditation and dream planes, just as he had met mine since I was a small boy. Each coil of the silver cord from Swamy Nagananda was also sealing in a spiritual *siddhi*—a God-given spiritual power. The *siddhis* are traditional spiritual powers, such as telepathy, clairvoyance, levitation, bi-location, teleportation, telekinesis, materialization and physical, emotional and spiritual healing. From childhood, I'd been blessed with many of these *siddhis*. I experienced telepathy when I was still in grade school; clairvoyance and levitation when I was in the military; materialization and healing from my early thirties on. I understood at that moment that in order to be pure all the *siddhis* I had been blessed with were explicitly to be used for the spiritual service of others. *Siddhis* must come as blessings for selfless spiritual effort. If they're sought as a way to wield power, they're impure—and exist in service of the ego. I had never worked to acquire *any* of the *siddhis*; they all just came to me. The *siddhis* operate from the laws of grace and karma to uplift and benefit others when karma justifies.

Siddhis are not to be demonstrated as stunts, like fire-walking, brick-breaking, sword swallowing or lying on a bed of nails. They are not to be displayed for show. If they are, seekers lose their focus on God as they waste time in fascination with developing powers. Natural *siddhis* are like blossoming flowers. They happen spontaneously as the result of God's love. The *siddhis* are Maya—illusions—and they can only further strengthen one's belief in Maya. The goal of the spiritual master is not to show people *siddhis*, but rather to turn people Godward—to the Self that resides within. When *siddhis* do happen spontaneously, they operate by their own laws, beyond the laws of time and space. They come through the master, from God. Their purpose is to transmit blessings.

Nagananda grew smaller and smaller while flying toward Babaji until he was just a blue dot entering Babaji's third eye. The ability to get smaller and smaller is another *siddhi*. I experienced Nagananda's astral body just as powerfully as if he were physically present. Whenever he has come to me in dreams—from 1962 until the present—this has always been the case. He appeared real, alive—as if I could reach out and touch him. Again, this takes place in the alternative reality, a dimension more real than this world. It always dissolves this "real" world into the larger reality of the spiritual dimension, like a cube of sugar thrown into the ocean. One need only be prepared to have this experience.

Babaji smiled, or rather, I noticed he was still smiling, clearly sharing the vision with me. As I looked at his smile, his face began to morph and his hair began to grow until the being that sat in front of me was none other than Swamy Yogananda, my first Guru. Babaji's smile was Yogananda's smile and Yogananda's smile was Babaji's. I now understood the peacefulness with which Yogananda had died. When he died he was communicating with Babaji.

For many months Yogananda had confidently told his disciples on which day he would depart his physical body. When the day came, he told them that he was going to give a final spiritual talk. The great master spoke for one hour. At the conclusion, he folded his hands together in the *Namaste position*[9] as his body gently slumped to the floor. At the moment of his departure, he smiled sweetly. Through his action he was telling us not to fear death. The body is only a suit of clothes that, sooner or later, the soul discards.

Now as I saw Yogananda, I understood that Babaji had guided my entire life. The experiences I had regarded as mistakes were the complex working out of karma; the steps necessary to bring me to this moment. As I looked in gratitude to Yogananda, I was experiencing his name; Yoga—ananda, the bliss of Yoga, or "union with the divine."

Yogananda's features transformed once again into those of the young Babaji. Babaji stepped down from his swing and approached me. He made a rapid circular motion with his hand, and streams of golden white light, in the form of *shakti* and *vibhuti*, rained down upon my head. I could see Babu *pranaming* at Babaji's feet. In his hands, Babu held the Krishna statue from the Ambassador. I saw Babaji make the motion to materialize something and hand it to Babu. Babu's face was radiating contentment.

From my right side I noticed an elderly white-robed being approaching with great dignity. This person was also preceded by blue light. It was the *Pope*!

I was startled and astonished to witness Babaji's divine relationship and communion even with the Pope. His Holiness shuffled through a doorway that led into a huge cathedral. I couldn't see into the cathedral, but I could hear the sound of thousands chanting in angelic voices. Again, I recognized this as the music of Creation.

I felt another strong breeze and noticed the blue dots were dispersing in every direction. The breeze had caused a leaf above me to fall freely down toward the ground. As I saw this, there was an in-rush of breath through my nose and mouth and a startling, snore-like noise. I snapped back into my body. This was not uncomfortable, but my body did not feel the same. It was remade of light and spiritual grace. I was totally at peace and had no desire to do anything. I certainly didn't want to move or get up.

I noticed that it was now dark. We had arrived around two o'clock in the afternoon. The fallen leaf lay in front of me. I picked it up and held it affectionately, as a reminder of the experience. Babaji was nowhere in sight. Two men were nearby. One offered me a drink of water from a ladle that came from a nearby pot. I politely refused, because I wasn't in a realm where I had any needs. I was not thirsty. And I noticed that I no longer needed a restroom.

"Where's Babaji?" I asked. The men pointed to indicate he was no longer in the courtyard, but inside the temple. I took the leaf back to the cab outside the compound. Babu was curled up like a cat in the front seat, sound asleep. The Krishna statue was gripped tightly in his hand. I carefully placed the leaf in the back seat, and then quietly walked away from the cab so as not to awaken him.

Because it was now dark, I wondered where I would be spending the night. Clearly, this temple was not inhabited and lacked any formal area for sleeping. In modern India the temple priest often has another job, and attends to the temple only occasionally. In days past, the government helped to keep the traditions and temple culture alive by subsidizing the priests. During this trip to India I saw temple walls "decorated" with posters of Hollywood sex symbols featuring seductive advertisements of new movies. This temple was remote enough that it was free of such desecration.

I walked across the courtyard and up the short flight of steps to the entrance of the temple. Outside, there was a little statue of *Ganesha*—the elephant deity who represents God's omnipotence. I was full of inner contentment and peace. A clear shift had taken place within me.

Before I could enter the temple, two men quickly approached me. They had a container of water and wanted me to wash my feet and hands before going inside. Smoke was pouring out the temple door. A fire was burning inside. Along with the smoke were the sounds of Sanskrit mantras being chanted.

As I entered, my stomach knotted up in panic. I suddenly felt like a child who had lost his parent. Where was Babaji? I wondered if he had left the temple. What if this mystical being had disappeared from my life just as inexplicably as he had entered it? The panic increased. I didn't know what to do. Was I expected to get into the car and return to the Windsor Manor? Was Babaji finished with me?

I became distracted. In the back of the temple hall was an alabaster statue of Krishna playing his flute. It was not only life-sized but life-like. At that moment, I realized Babu had, in fact, brought me to a Krishna temple. My eyes were drawn to several swamis sitting around the fire. They were wearing bright orange *lungis*—the simple cloth wraps so common in India—and necklaces of the sacred *rudraksha*[10] beads. One of the swamis was cleanly shaven and leading the others in a chant. These were no ordinary swamis. Their eyes were ablaze with spiritual fire. I had never seen such liquid eyes. The light poured out of them. I noticed their *lungis*[11] were silk; not the typical plain cotton. Normally swamis only wear silk on holy days. What was the occasion?

As I observed the situation, I recognized one of Hinduism's oldest spiritual rituals—the elements of the *homa*—a fire ceremony performed to cleanse and purify the temple atmosphere and the surrounding area.

"This ceremony will spread your name far and wide," Babaji said, materializing next to me out of nowhere. As I was entranced by the radiance of the swamy's eyes, I jumped at his sudden arrival. Had he picked that precise moment to teleport himself next to me, or was it a coincidence that I had been distracted? Spiritual masters do not like to make a display of their powers. I knew he had teleported, because there was only one entrance to the temple, and I would have seen him approach through it. I had been anxiously awaiting his return, and was constantly checking.

Babaji motioned for me to take a seat on the white concrete floor near the fire. He was wearing a large *rudraksha* necklace. *Rudraksha* beads bring blessings because they are highly sensitive transmitters of divine energy. I also noticed a pleasing jasmine scent coming from his body. I had noticed it around him when we were outside as well. He motioned for me to sit, and I did so immediately and silently—like a "soldier." I was more than happy to do whatever he wanted. But he didn't join me, and simply walked away. I could clearly hear his soft footfalls upon the floor of the temple. He did not say how long I was to sit, or when he would return. No problem, I thought. I am in God's hands.

As I sat in the temple, I focused my eyes upon the fire and upon the main priest, or *pujari*. The fire was so close and so intense that I became damp with perspiration. Smoke billowed out insistently, directly into my face, burning my eyes and choking me. After a couple of minutes, I made several polite attempts to move to different locations around the fire. But, no matter where I moved, the smoke followed, winding its way toward me like a "snake-cloud," as if it were alive and searching for me. Uncomfortable as I was, this living smoke was fascinating.

An older, gray-haired, bearded swamy with a kind face, motioned for me to sit still. I was in the inner circle, surrounded by the swamis, so I made the effort. I didn't want to behave improperly during the ceremony. Nonetheless, my eyes continued to burn as my face and hands became covered with soot. The gray-haired swamy indicated with gestures that I should use my cupped hands to direct the smoke toward the top of my head and to my heart.

"This is no ordinary smoke. It is alive and is the offering of Mother Agni to you. Blessings," he said.

Agni, the ancient fire goddess, is invoked to bring the blessings of purification. My eyes closed involuntarily and I focused my awareness gently into my third eye. Within moments, I was transported, once again, to the golden white light realm of *Premananda*. How fantastic! It was similar to my earlier encounter with Babaji in that both the swamis and the *puja* fire were present identically on two dimensions. One was the outer world, and the other was *Premananda*, the inner universe.

In *Premananda* the smoke and heat were not bothering me at all. Here the smoke was silvery blue in color, and it was indeed alive. Like the wind, this so-called "smoke" was a form of intelligent energy. I thought immediately of Native American traditions of honoring smoke as sacred, and the Hindu custom of using an abundance of incense suddenly made sense.

I would never again look at my world in the same way. It was clear that there are many forms of intelligence in what I formerly thought of as random actions and events. Trees and plants are intelligent. Babaji chose to sit under the tree because he wanted the company of the tree's wisdom. He was in silent communication with the tree! Wind is intelligence. The sky is intelligent. The sun and moon are intelligent. They all are full of God's life force, or *prana*, and they are full of consciousness. The reality is that each of us lives within an infinite sea of God consciousness. Even objects we normally assume are inanimate are made of God stuff: God's *prana*.

I was startled out of blissful *Premananda* by the sound of a blaring horn and drum. When I opened my eyes I saw that this horn was a good seven feet long, and its sounds ripped the air and tore through my body. I'd once heard that Indian music is designed to open up our spiritual centers. I must admit, something was opening up in me. The long wooden hand drum was also loud, but softer, not so jarring as the horn. It seemed odd to me that I hadn't noticed the instruments as I entered the temple.

Now the lead swamy was pouring some liquid onto the fire. I think it was *ghee*, a sweet clarified butter used in Indian cooking and fire ceremonies. I felt somewhat out of place in my Western clothing—like a cowboy attending a black tie soiree in dirty dungarees and boots. I felt no reproach from the swamis, just my own fleeting discomfort in reaction to an inner picture of how it could be different, how it "should" look. I chastised myself for complaining.

Wasn't the moment perfect enough? How many perfect moments had I ignored in my frantic search for an even better moment, or the next moment? Always so caught up in our stuff, we often fail to perceive the miracle we are in. Much of my life had been lived in this fashion.

I think most of us are so uncomfortable with ourselves that we spend much of our time in distractions, barely aware of the moment we are passing through. We distract ourselves with food, snacking between meals on tea, sodas, a cookie or some ice cream. We keep ourselves busy lighting a cigarette or cigar, chewing gum, biting our nails. We fiddle with the radio controller, anxious to find just the right music because without the music, how can we have a good moment? When we can't think of anything else to do we urgently check our email or pick up the telephone and try to pull someone else into our moment.

We also distract ourselves from the moment by living in the past or planning for the future. For many, daydreaming is a skillful form of escapism. Whether we realize it or not, we can't face the moment because we're starving for the most important nourishment. Our constant hunger is for "love." We want to feel love and be loved. What we've missed is that satiety comes not in the receiving but in the giving.

This is it. *This* is the moment. The glory and love of God is here in this moment. Heaven is in this moment. Enlightenment is in this very moment. *This is it!* If we don't learn here and *now* to appreciate it, what will ever satisfy us? A man arrives in heaven and complains, "How can we enjoy this harp music without some Ben and Jerry's ice cream?"

In the middle of winter, St. Francis of Assisi turned to the wisdom of an almond tree and asked it to reveal God to him. In response, the tree blossomed. God is aliveness. God exists fully in this moment, and it is up to us to face the moment fully to find God. St. Francis' life was full of miracles because he searched for God intently *in the moment.* Where else could God be? In 1997 an earthquake in Italy destroyed the Cathedral of St. Francis. Miraculously, the delicate frescoes depicting his life were all spared. The Divine Intelligence wanted those frescoes spared.

The old bearded swamy placed a jasmine flower garland around my neck. I felt a little awkward, wishing I had flowers to place upon him and his companions in return. I wasn't yet fully aware that this ceremony was happening on *my* behalf.

Finally, after about forty minutes, Babaji returned. Whenever he entered the room I could physically feel the spiritual vibrations elevate. Activities seemed to speed up, yet somehow simultaneously slow down. I felt both more invigorated and more relaxed.

Babaji held a brown coconut in each of his hands. Standing next to the clean-shaven swamy, he skillfully banged the two coconuts together, opening both, and poured their liquid into the fire.

"Whatsoever the *Avatar* wills, no earthly person or situation can undo. This removes the old life. No longer same on the inside," he said.

Babaji grew quiet and began rotating his hand in a quick, circular fashion. *Vibhuti* again came from his palm and he offered it to the fire. The flames leapt upward toward his hands to receive the divine gift. He let the flames lick his fingertips. A sweet smile played upon his face, as if he were allowing his favorite puppy to lick him joyfully. The elements of nature were Babaji's beloved children.

"*Vibhuti* is a symbol of God's grace." Babaji's eyes were not on me. He was still interacting with the fire. "Creation comes from *vibhuti*. It is God's clay."

"Take some ash from the fire," Babaji said. I looked into the fire and saw mostly glowing coals. Did he want me to pick up coals? I wondered. Marilyn, Beau and I once attended a workshop taught by Tolly Burkan—the founder of the American Firewalking Movement—in Northern California. We walked on fire for eight days to achieve certification as fire-walking instructors. For some reason, I had been compelled to go beyond the walk on 1,200 degree coals that the other participants were trying to master. In addition to walking, I needed to literally pick the coals up, and walk around with them in my hand. No one, including me, could understand why I kept doing this. At this moment I sensed that the experience had been preparation for what Babaji was asking me to do.

Babaji was actually telling me to get some ash, not pick up coals. But, how could I get ash if not from the hot, glowing coals? Did he know I had handled coals before? Did he want me to pick up coals to learn that I could do it without ego-enhancing motives? Did he want me to become friends with Agni, the fire goddess, in the same playful way that he was?

"Problem?" he asked.

Clearly, I was taking too long to act, spending too much time in my mind. The way he said, "Problem?" suggested there should be no problem. My last thought in this moment of hesitation was that I should use my left hand. If I *was* going to get burned, I was only going to burn one hand—the one I didn't use as much. I exhaled, plunged my hand into the edge of the fire bed, and scooped up a coal the size of a lime along with a handful of black ash.

I winced, overreacting in anticipation, as I felt the fire singe some hairs on my wrist. At first, my hand felt nothing—no heat—just the weight of the embers. After a few seconds I felt the sting of heat. I didn't dare let the coals go, because Babaji was looking at me, and I didn't want to fail this test. If he wanted me to burn my hand, then I assumed it would be for my own good, perhaps burning off some personal karma. Whatever was happening, I knew it was some kind of test.

Suddenly, the sting became cool. It was uncanny, but there was no time to think about it, as Babaji was on the move, motioning me to follow. The horn blared ear-piercing farewells as we left the temple. I bowed to each of the swamis on my way out. I followed Babaji outside and around to the back of the temple, where we entered a small room. It had a dirt floor and, on one wall, there was a small barred window. In former days, it had clearly been used as sleeping quarters for the temple priest. In the center of the room a small fire burned in a low pit. This fireplace was designed to provide warmth, but it obviously served as a kitchen and a source of light as well.

Cobwebs were in abundance. I carefully moved around them, putting my newfound understanding to work. These were the homes of intelligent beings! The mere sight of a cobweb in the past would have sent me into a mild—and sometimes not so mild—anxiety attack. At that particular moment, I couldn't have cared less. I noticed this change, one of many to come.

Babaji motioned for me to sit on the dirt floor in the tiny kitchen.

"There are many bad men in America," he stated. "They look for shortcuts to spirituality." I wondered if he thought I had forgotten what he'd previously said, or if he was repeating himself to be sure his words were impressed upon my consciousness.

"If someone wants power of materialization, they do *Gayatri Mantra*, Tch!...one hour a day for fifteen years. But this horrible waste of time. Imagine what soul would accomplish, if meditation on God one hour a day for fifteen years!

"Not Krishna's goal that one should materialize. Krishna's whole message about this one issue: find God, love God, serve God, remember God. Time waste is life waste.

"People who take shortcuts to materialize and other *siddhis* will come to America. They try to compete with gifts and *siddhis* I give you from time you were child. I warn Europe and America—not be fooled. These are not men and women of God. They all business and show."

I knew what Babaji was warning me about. Materializations had begun to come through me several years earlier in 1988. Since that time, I'd been known for my ability to materialize *vibhuti* and many other sacred gifts, although I never did this on demand and usually tried as hard as I could to avoid any public display. Babaji was warning that some of the spiritual messengers in our country were working hard to *acquire* the *siddhis* as egoic merit badges. *Siddhis* carry with them the requirement that we have discipline and discrimination. As "miracles" *siddhis* are unimportant; the whole world is a miracle. So, in fact, there are no miracles at all—only the beauty and mystery of life.

"Babaji, I don't think most Westerners want to hear this message of mysticism and miracles. They are very busy with climbing the corporate ladder and making a 'better life' for themselves. They have their hands full with children and the demands of work and social life." I painfully reflected on the resistance that I had experienced for many decades, as I tried to move people toward a path of higher consciousness. Materializations had actually scared people away from my message, and I recently found myself trying to *suppress* them when they came. As I sat there with Babaji, I felt renewed clarity that the only mission I had was to lead people to an experience of their own divinity.

He looked at me as if I hadn't understood a word. "Yes, always souls who want only to make the senses happy. There also those who don't want to grow spiritually. These souls choosing many more lifetimes of learning God's lessons hard way. True Yoga a sacred path, revealed only to spiritually mature. Krishna comes to old souls ready to awaken to deepen spiritual life they start in past lives. Many such souls in America."

"I agree. There are now many Americans who practice Hatha Yoga in the United States," I offered, "especially in California."

"Baba not talking about people standing on head and stretching to feel good. Talking about immersion in complete science of spirituality. Krishna will send many old souls to you," he repeated.

Inwardly, I wondered how many Americans would actually

be ready for the message of reincarnation that Babaji was stating as fact. Interestingly, about four-fifths of the world's population believes in reincarnation. Reincarnation was even an accepted fact of Christianity, until it was excised from the Bible at the Council of Trent in the fifth century.

"This is time of Yogis," Babaji continued. "Many young will hear this message. They come to you. It possible to live in world, meditate, follow peaceful yogic lifestyle. Young people are old souls; they have hunger for spiritual depth. Want to experience God. Not satisfied with churches of their parents. Want their own spiritual centers for congregation. They help you build ashrams in West. Ashrams will be modern temples for people of all religions to lay aside prejudice and welcome all travelers on God's highways."

Babaji stopped and materialized a handful of *vibhuti*. "This for Greg," he said.

"For his health?" I asked.

His look said yes, and for so much more, as he gave that characteristic Indian waggle of the head that said everything and nothing. He started to hand me the ash, but realized that my left hand was full of the embers. He called out in Hindi, and moments later when one of the swamis entered, Babaji spoke to him in clipped, sing-song Hindi. The swamy left, and a short time later returned with a sheet of paper. Babaji put Greg's *vibhuti* on the paper and folded it up to make a packet.

"*Vibhuti* very powerful. Use like medicine. One speck bring better results than handful if used with proper respect," Babaji said.

"What is the proper way?"

"Take tiny amount with this finger," he held up the ring finger of his right hand. "Take little bit and place on forehead. Remember God inside."

"Babaji, how will Americans know if someone who displays the powers is a spiritual force for good? And will *you* be coming to America?" I asked. I was elated for Greg and couldn't wait to call him and tell him about the *vibhuti*. Babaji placed the package on the floor next to me.

"Babaji not take physical form to America. Too many sex and beer vibrations. This holy body needs spiritual vibrations, come from the thousands of years of spiritual worship in this sacred land. Babaji's body India's body. America the land of TV and vibrations are wrong. America land of Geraldo and Oprah. (He pronounced it, "Jur-all-dough, like Geronimo.) Americans become used to diet of sensationalism and have strong hunger for dark news which TV feeds."

" Geraldo, " I said, emphasizing the correct pronunciation.

"Who?" Babaji asked.

"Geraldo... Hair-rahl-doe," I pronounced. "I think you said "Jur-all-dough."

"Hair-rahl-doe is good man, but he needs take responsibility for the TV. This man has had powerful spiritual experiences," Babaji said. I assumed Babaji meant that Geraldo needed to take responsibility for his programs. I wondered why he had pronounced Geraldo's name incorrectly. Later, I would come to understand that he did this to insure that I would remember the conversation.

"Babaji empowering you to carry my message for New Age. This your task. I not speak through other voices. How can there be any confusion? They know you by your love and by the loving works you do," he said.

I wondered if he meant New Age or New Millennium. "Do you mean the New Millennium?" I asked. I was overwhelmed by the enormity of his comment. I had not had time to fully absorb it. It was difficult to think of questions, but I knew I had some, and so I just asked whatever came to mind.

"New Age, New Millennium... same," he said.

"People will have questions, Babaji."

"I give you answers."

"Hold your hand out," Babaji commanded.

I stretched forth the hand that contained the coals and black soot.

"Who is your favorite God?"

My mind raced through several possibilities: Jesus, Buddha, Krishna...

I decided upon *Shiva*, the original Guru. The Guru is the one who brings you to moments like this.

"Shiva," I said.

Babaji smiled and told me to close my hand over the coals. He placed his hand over my hand and I fell into a deep meditative swoon, with eyes wide open. My ears were pounding and the room was flooded with golden light. The feeling reminded me of the times I'd been knocked out while boxing or while being thrown hard to the ground in judo, except I was not feeling any pain. There was a flash of lightning over our hands, which momentarily lit up the room, and Babaji removed his hand.

"Open it," he said.

I slowly opened my hand and gazed into my palm. A clear, luminescent, egg-shaped crystal lay in my palm. There were no coals, nor traces of black soot. Only a tiny amount of gray ash and white *vibhuti*. I loved it. The whole world was in that egg-shaped crystal. My mind could never fathom what secrets it held.

I quickly took the object in my right hand and held it up excitedly. Babaji looked mortified.

"Careful!" he commanded. "It not cooled yet."

My index finger and thumb of my right hand were quickly speaking to me of horrendous pain...burning pain. The egg-shaped object was *hot*! And it was molten, still soft. I saw to my dismay that it was dented where I had squeezed it. I quickly transferred it back to my left palm. As it cooled, it remained dented.

"Look at it! Look deeply into it!" he urged.

This was not difficult, as the object had a pale silvery luminescence that magnetically drew my stare.

"It is alive," he whispered, his voice hushed.

As I gazed, my eyes were drawn into its center, into its inner world of golden white light. Again I saw a lightning flash and many images of birth, mostly the heads of babies as they emerged from their mothers' wombs. I also saw flowers, especially roses blossoming quickly as in time-lapse photography. I had frequently seen roses materialize that same way in my hand and open in the same manner.

"It's so small," I commented stupidly. I wasn't complaining. I was completely awestruck. I noticed a soft white light was pulsating from the egg.

"No thinking! Stop! Look!" Babaji urged.

As I gazed upon the egg-shaped crystal, it was expanding. Soon it included the entire temple and more—a universe in its own right. Inside I saw Babaji's face, only he had long hair and looked very much like the drawing in Yogananda's autobiography. He stayed like this for a moment, and then I had the most surreal experience. His face became a collection of race, age and gender. A portion of his head and hair was Anglo feminine, another was male African, American Indian female, Grecian nose, almond-shaped eyes that changed colors—brown, black, blue, green. Different parts of his face were different colors: brown, black, yellow, red, white. His face was

are many false prophets in the world and they have voice of millions. They are pompous shadows of arrogance...parade their knowledge of brass and trash. My devotees will know them by their lack of humility before the presence of Guru. I will send devotees to protect you and Marilyn. They will come swiftly like angels. Fear not the dark for they too serve Baba's purpose. Whenever Babaji turns his sankalpa—his spiritual will—to problem, it vanishes."

Babaji placed his hand over my heart and rubbed it in a circular fashion. His hand felt hot.

"As you do this to other men, you send Babaji's love and open up their heart *chakras.* Touch women gently on face or shoulder, and this have same effect."

As he continued the motion, tears began to flow down my face. It was as if a dam had burst...lifetimes of devotion poured from my heart. These were the tears of lifetimes of yearning for God.

"*Bhakti*[14] tears. These tears for purification of others...many others will be led into the light of God. Krishna[15] will bless."

Babaji began to sing...

Om	the sound of creation
Purnamadah	That is the Holy
Purnamidam	This is the Holy
Purnat purnamudaachyate	The Holy births the Holy
Purnasya purnamadaya	Holy comes from the Holy
Purnameva vashisyate	And Holy still remains

Babaji sang this verse three times. He wanted me to understand it. I knew he wanted me to *use it.* He sang it in Sanskrit and then translated. The above is my best recollection of it.

He went on. "This from the *ISA* (eesah) *Upanishad. Upanishad* means sit at feet of master. This is true *Upanishad.*

The West needs to have *Upanishad* and so I send you to them. The *ISA Upanishad* is sacred book more than 5,000 years old. If you remember the song, it is enough. It bring forth a new *Upanishad* for West. You now carry this *Upanishad* within you. Just as *rishis*[16] were whispered the *Vedas*[17] in days past, so, too, will I whisper to you wisdom when needed. Because you carry this *Upanishad* within you, like a mother with child. I will protect you. I will send my drivers and others to protect. My angels are many. The sapling must be fenced."

Strangely, at that moment, my mid-section swelled forward several inches, as a tremendous amount of heat radiated from my solar plexus. It would remain swollen for the rest of my time in India, even though I lost more than fifteen pounds. Babaji had compared my condition to pregnancy, and now I truly looked pregnant. As I became the carrier of this *Upanishad*, it manifested in my physical body as *prana*. Months later in the United States, when I found it necessary to purchase a new pair of shoes, I found my feet had grown a full inch. I now wear shoes a size larger than I've ever worn in my life. Foot growth in an adult is typical of one known condition: *pregnancy*.

Babaji compared me to a sapling. "I have created you without bark so you most easily carry the Krishna light. You are now like mirror," he added. "I send sweet people for your company. You touching others will bring spiritual blessings to them."

"You are a good person, Babaji," I said, as the child I had become in his presence. It was hard to find words after all that had transpired, and this is all that I could muster.

"You, too. You will find best success when you talk about God. Help others to find God." Babaji nodded his head and his

photo of
Babaji
materialized
for Dionslo

dust devil

was upon us, and Babu and I were quickly rolling up all our windows. Leaves were swirling upward with the cloud. I couldn't follow the path of the flurry, and lost track of it in the darkness above. Looking back at the temple, I lost my breath as I realized it was absolutely dark. Vacant.

"Swamiji is happy with Krishna temple?" Babu interrupted my awe.

"Yes, very happy," I said.

We started to pick up speed, leaving only a cloud of dust behind us in the pitch-black night. The sky was brilliant with its many stars. As I looked upward, I remembered a Christmas Eve long ago when I searched the sky for Santa Claus's sled. I remembered the moment vividly. My cheek was pressed up against the cold window as I looked hopefully up into the Arizona sky for any sign of Santa's sleigh. I could feel my brothers next to me in the back seat of Dad's old Ford Fairlane, going up Main Street toward our home. At this moment, on this night, I felt very much as I had then.

During the long drive that followed, Babu made a few stops at village truck stops so he could get coffee or tea. I noticed that, unlike other taxi drivers in India, Babu didn't smoke. He offered me water, which I continued to refuse. I felt absolutely no desire for refreshment of any kind. I had no bodily needs at all. The time with Babaji had lifted me to his high state of *breathairianism.* At this moment, I was living completely on air. At one of our stops, I took a sip of Indian coffee out of courtesy because Babu had kindly purchased it for me.

I slept for most of the journey back. When I wasn't sleeping, I was meditating or repeating mantras.[19] At one point Babu pulled over, and we both slept for a little while. We were exhausted.

The darkness faded into morning. Bleary-eyed, I watched the Indian countryside pass by. It is always amazing to watch

India come to life. I especially enjoyed watching the farmers emerge and head for their fields. I loved the schoolchildren, coming out of shanties alongside the road, neat in their pressed navy blue uniforms. Everyone who was moving along the road appeared to be smiling at me—the men and women, the children, even the cows, *especially the cows.* They all seemed to notice me. Even the clouds seemed to be taking shape just for me, to entertain me. Everything was part of the Show of the Universe—and the whole cast was in on the fact, and had awakened to the vast drama they were enacting.

Gradually the villages became towns and I knew we were approaching Bangalore. The nearer we came to the city, the more convincing the actors and actresses became—and the more oblivious to the show. Graffiti began to appear between enormous posters advertising Hollywood's latest. The poster for *Natural Born Killers* struck me as particularly offensive. Now this brutal film, widely promoted in India, was inundating some of the sweetest and most innocent people in the world with images of brutality and fear. What were we Americans doing? It seemed like madness.

As we approached Bangalore the atmosphere itself became more and more stifling and unpleasant. The unchecked use of lead gasoline meant that emissions polluted the air, making it difficult to breathe. Everywhere were people wearing face masks or bandanas tied around their mouths. The least fortunate of the population used their hands to try to keep the invading fumes from destroying their lungs.

I bent down to search for my Birkenstocks. For the first time since leaving Babaji, I looked down at myself, and I realized how filthy I was. I was completely covered with black filthy

Bubu
taxi
disappears

never saw him again

to pay him $300

not enjoyed

PETALS FROM THE LOTUS

"I'm wanting the Babu taxi," I said to the doorman the next day.

After my encounter with Babaji, I frequently found myself communicating in Indian English. He had set in motion a process of change, and a personality shift was immediately apparent. With hotel clerks, shopkeepers, tellers in the bank—with educated Indians or Westerners I encountered—I often took on the role of a buffoon or simpleton, a misguided "Western Spiritual Seeker." With the open-hearted Indian people, I would reach out in great love and tenderness, involuntarily communicating the vibrations of Babaji. This reflected his love of the simplicity and genuineness of those he called the "sweet people."

None of this was in my control. Babaji was teaching me that "I" was not my mind, personality or what we call ego. He was coming through me, and I became comfortable with him using my mind and body. I had fully surrendered to him and the ancient alchemical transformation he was performing. Not only were my shoes uncomfortable but by the time I returned to the United States a month later I had ballooned from

Still asking
for "Krishna" Babu
taxi driver

takes "Shena" Tsalson

driver who is older

shee not staying more

than 480 in one place

Cab drivers in India operate with amazing efficiency. I was impressed that Babu knew who I was.

"*Namaste*," I replied.

His smile was kindly. The gleaming gold Star of David hanging from his neck struck me as unusual.

"Do you mind me asking why you are wearing a Star of David?" I asked.

"I am Jewish. I come from Kerala. Many Jewish Indians there, sir. You wish to go to Kerala? Very nice there, sir. Much nicer than Bangalore."

Babu seemed familiar somehow, as if I'd known him for a long time. A horn blared from behind, signaling us to move on.

"All right," I said, "take me to Kerala." I was trusting that Babaji's cosmic travel agency would send me where I needed to be.

"That's good incense," I commented. It was particularly sweet and, unlike much of the incense I encountered in India, didn't burn my eyes or make me choke.

"Yes, it is Shiva incense. You like Shiva?" he queried.

"Yes."

My throat tightened with emotion as I fondly recalled Babaji at that moment. My eyes misted with tears as I beheld his image in my mind's eye. I was holding the Shiva power object in my left hand, and could feel it pulsating like a heart.

"Where are you, Babaji?" my heart cried out. The Shiva power object pulsed again. As it did, the center of my chest pulsed in unison.

"Shiva is powerful god. He is destroyer of all that is evil," Babu explained. "We go to Shiva statue, then to Kerala."

"How can you be Jewish and worship Shiva, Babu?" I asked. "Don't you believe that there is only one God?"

"Shiva is a *symbol* of the one God," he responded, smiling light-heartedly.

I could no longer talk. My eyes were closed as I contemplated Babaji.

"Next week the Dalai Lama is coming," said Babu. "He is going to visit the Shiva monument. I hope it will give him the power to get those Chinese out of his country. Shiva lives in Tibet." He said this as if Shiva were a living being, as real as the Dalai Lama.

We drove through Bangalore for about thirty minutes, winding along the curves and tree-lined expanses of Sankey Road, built by the English decades earlier. It was horribly congested with bullock carts, rickshaws, motorcycles, monkeys, bicycles, buses, cars and pedestrians all moving in a slow flow with no lanes. Thick toxic black fumes billowed everywhere, making the air impossible to breathe. All around me I saw people wearing surgical face masks or pressing handkerchiefs over their mouths in vain efforts to protect themselves from India's increasingly insidious pollution. My heart broke at what runaway development and "advancement" were doing to this ancient land.

"Roll up the windows and put the air conditioner on," I suggested to Babu. He waggled his head affirmatively and did what I asked.

After about ten minutes, with the cab getting hotter and hotter, I realized that the air conditioner wasn't working. The car was indeed equipped with an air conditioner, for which I would pay extra. It was a technical detail that it wasn't functional.

"Let's turn the air conditioner off, and just open the window," I pleaded. Babu looked hurt.

Minutes later, we pulled up to the park that contained the Shiva statue. It was a new monument, perhaps a year old, which was as large as a medium-sized office building. I immediately was overwhelmed by the force field of energy it radiated. I was surprised to see how few people were around. This confirmed what I'd already noticed: in this era, Indians spend more time at the Western food franchises and the bars and nightclubs than at worship. At this remarkable shrine, I saw only a few gardeners and maintenance people tending to the grounds.

"They are making it ready for the Dalai Lama," Babu said. A young Indian girl wearing a burnt orange sari came up to the Ambassador and held up *malas*, or flower garlands.

"Dr. Donald, you must buy. Never wise to approach Shiva with empty hands," Babu instructed.

I took one white *mala*, but Babu motioned to the girl to give me the full dozen or more strands she was carrying. She smiled and handed the entire set to me. I handed her thirty rupees and could tell by her look that this was more than enough. She skipped off down the street with the rupees in hand. I watched her approach a ragged woman, old-looking beyond her years, who was breastfeeding a baby in the street. Two naked toddlers tugged at her faded cotton sari. The flower girl handed her the rupees, and the mother bowed in my direction. I pulled more rupees from my pocket and walked over to her. She gestured with her hand toward her mouth to indicate she needed food. Her lips were cracked with malnutrition, and her ribs poked out from beneath her choli, the cropped blouse she wore beneath her sari. It was then that I noticed her left foot was badly mangled.

The two toddlers were covered with dirt and both were crying. I again reached into my pocket and pulled out an entire roll of rupees and gave them to her. As she took them in her shaking hand, she fell to her knees, one arm holding onto my leg as she wept. I started crying too, and instinctively reached forward and touched the top of her head with the Shiva crystal.

There was a golden flash of light, and I felt a hot current flow into the top of the woman's head. The light startled several crows who cawed loudly as they flew away. I realized that the toddlers had abruptly stopped crying.

"Come, sir." It was Babu. He gently pulled the sobbing woman away from me. Her face, wet with tears, was ecstatic. Her jaw had dropped, and she was staring intently at the Shiva statue.

"You must wear these flowers," said Babu, placing a garland of jasmine around my neck. "A swamy like you should wear flowers." The sweet fragrance filled my nostrils.

"Hurry, sir. Shiva is waiting," he urged.

I glanced at my watch. It was exactly 11:00 A.M.

"Wait a minute, Babu! Did you call me Swamy?"

"Yes, Swamiji."

"Why are you calling me that?"

"My rabbi told me that today I would be traveling with a swamy. He knows these things," Babu said, matter-of-factly.

I couldn't have looked less like an Indian swamy, who would typically have been dressed in orange. I was wearing chinos, Birkenstocks, and a white button-down shirt. On the pocket flap was an embroidered brown teddy bear wearing a blue vest. When I'd arrived in Los Angeles from Australia only a few days earlier all I had were the dark suits and dress shirts I used for public appearances for the *Fitonics* book tour with Marilyn. But since these weren't suitable for the heat of India, Marilyn and I had rushed to the mall hours before my plane took off to find lighter, more casual clothes. We quickly bought three of these white shirts, and it was only when I opened them the next morning in New York that I realized to my dismay that I'd be traveling through India with a teddy bear insignia on my chest. I had no other shirts! In time, I would grow to love my teddy bears and feel naked without them.

My Birkenstock sandals, acquired in the same hurried pre-flight shopping spree, were also an ironic item. I'd always resisted Birkenstocks and joked about them as an icon of "sixties spirituality." But I had to admit they were quite comfortable, and when Babaji saw them, he loved them.

"But I don't look like a swamy," I protested to Babu.

"Swamy is more than clothes, sir. It is the heart. You have the heart of Swamy," Babu commented.

Only two days had passed since I'd learned from Nagananda that I was to be initiated as a swamy, and already three people had taken me for one.

"What mystery is this?" I wondered.

The giant statue of Shiva beckoned. An old Brahmin priest approached, and motioned me to take my sandals off. I handed them to Babu, who had already slipped off his rubber thongs. The priest smeared three lines of white ash across my forehead to honor Shiva. He also sprinkled perfumed "water" upon the top of my head. I heard Babu calling to someone in Hindi.

The priest motioned for me to follow him and we approached the statue. With a gesture, he directed me to a spot on the ground beneath a tree, where I could sit and meditate. Before I could sit, an old woman approached carrying a palm frond, and swept the area he'd indicated.

I started to sit, but Babu stopped me.

"Wait, sir," he implored. His hands were full of white flower petals.

"You must offer Shiva petals from the lotus flower. Then meditation is good."

He placed the soft delicate petals into my hand.

"When I am in the West, and I want to honor Shiva, how do I do so without lotus petals?" I asked. I was thinking of the Shiva crystal I carried.

"One must offer the petals from one's heart," Babu replied. I nodded and turned to face the gigantic statue.

"The priest says there is one more thing," said Babu, "One must give donation."

I lay the petals down on the ground and followed the two men. At the entrance to the park was a collection box for donations. I reached into my pocket for rupees and started to put them into the box, but once again Babu stopped me.

"You must make dream."

"Dream?"

"Wash. Big wash!"

"Wash?" I asked.

"Yes, big wash to Shiva."

For a peculiar moment, I thought I was somehow donating money to help clean the statue. Then I realized I needed to make a wish.

"Dear Shiva, please bring my beloved Marilyn many blessings. Bless our romance and our marriage. Please protect our children," I prayed silently.

We returned to the meditation spot and I gathered the flower petals.

"Place the petals at Shiva's feet," Babu advised.

I held the petals for a moment next to my heart. "Please God, Lord Shiva, by whatever name or form you use, help me to be an instrument to bring people the profound peace and bliss you offer. Thank you for bringing me to Babaji."

I tossed them high into the air and watched them float down to earth beneath the statue.

A feeling of peace came into my body. I settled comfortably into a meditative posture on the cool Indian soil beneath the tree. Babu and the priest walked off together, leaving me alone.

"Acha! You must breathe, Swamiji!" the quiet sweet voice exhorted.

"Babaji!" I exclaimed.

I was eager to see him and my eyes flew open, my vision alighting on the white lotus petals arrayed around the cold, blue-gray base of the statue.

"Why trouble to look outside for what is inside?"

The voice was coming from my heart. I closed my eyes and, within, I could see Babaji sitting in his bamboo swing. He waved to me as he rocked back and forth. His wave created a whirlpool-like sensation that pulled me deep inside my chest, and I found that I was sitting at his feet.

"Tch. You must breathe," he said insistently.

"I *am* breathing," I replied.

"Not just outer breathing, but Inner Breathing. Inner Breathing is the key to immortality. What is immortal is real. What is mortal is false. You must begin to breathe like the immortal you are. Next breath is different."

I had been listening intently to every word, and I realized my breath was suspended. This is a natural human reaction. Concentrate and listen intently to some faraway noise and notice that you will automatically hold your breath.

"Babaji, I didn't know if I would ever see you again."

"Like Krishna drives the chariot, I drive your mind, body and ego. You can do nothing except that which Babaji wills. You are a swamy. *Swa* means surrender. True swamy is one who has surrendered all to be of service to the Divine. True Swamy is rare. Only a handful have this honor. Many wear the cloth of the priest, rabbi, monk, or the swamy, outer show only."

I felt white light come into the top of my head. It flowed like liquid mercury down the front of my spine with a pleasant cooling sensation. My jaw relaxed automatically as I inhaled through my mouth. A long, deep breath rushed down to my belly button, as my stomach relaxed. The air entered audibly in a slow, gentle snore-like sound. The liquid white light flowed down the front of my body—all the way down my trunk—where it reversed at the tailbone.

There it transformed into a warm golden light, and as I slowly exhaled, it traveled up my spine to the top of my head. I was automatically exhaling through my mouth, still making the quiet snoring sound.

Inwardly, I saw what looked like an open, inverted lily-white umbrella in the top of my head.

"Petals from the lotus," Babaji explained. "This is your crown *chakra*, your spiritual energy center."

As the warm golden light reached the inner lotus flower, ecstatic rushes flowed into the core of my being. Then the warm golden light again began a descent down the front of my body and, as it did, it cooled once more into the white silvery liquid.

"You will bring this Inner Breath to others. It burns off negative karma so they may grow spiritually. This Inner Breathing is the fastest way to God-Realization."[1]

Something inside me had been set into motion, like a lawnmower when its starter cord has been pulled and the engine kicks over and roars to life. There was a continuous circulation of the light within my body as it made one revolution after another. My outer breath followed the movement of the inner breath.

"Tch. This is how one becomes a living soul," Babaji explained. "Until one learns the inner breath, only body and mind...no soul...only potential. Soul takes birth through Inner Breathing..." his words faded away as the noise of my breathing drowned out his voice. I could see him rocking back and forth in his swing. Golden white light permeated every cell of my body. I was delirious with an indescribable joy.

"Marilyn likes to rock," his nectarine voice returned to me. I didn't know if it was a question or a statement.

"Rock?" I pictured my beloved with earphones on, strumming an electric guitar. This certainly wasn't Marilyn.

"No, Babaji. She likes classical, or spiritual music."

"No, not Marilyn. She likes all music," he insisted.

"Marilyn likes to rock," he stated again. I wasn't sure if it was a question or statement.

"*Rock*, Babaji?" I asked.

"Like this," he said, as he rocked more vigorously back and forth within his swing. "Rocking is good for Marilyn. It is good for all women. It helps to release the spiritual energy within the spine. Men too, but women and children more so."

"Marilyn likes trees?" Babaji asked. This was definitely a question.

"Yes, she needs trees," I responded.

"*Needs* trees!" He made it sound like a basic food group.

"Yes, she does need trees. Her father taught her to plant trees as a child. It is something she loved to do with her children when they were young."

"The world suffers because there are too few trees. God created, but man has destroyed. Where there are no trees the people perish.

"Inner Breathing most successful if done near plants or trees," Babaji continued. "It will slow down and reverse aging. Main benefit is God-realization."

My body and mind were in spiritual ecstasy. The warm golden light was soothing away all inner tension, while the cooling white liquid light was filling me with boundless inner energy.

"How is Emperor Clinton?" he asked. He had stopped swinging.

"Emperor Clinton? You mean President Clinton?" I asked.

He seemed miffed that I had corrected him.

"No, *Emperor*," he asserted. "More respect needs to be given to this station."

"You don't understand Americans, Babaji. They will never call a President an Emperor."

"Emperor and Empress Clinton will suffer much from the Jackass in the coming year."

"Jackass?"

"The Repooblicans."

"Oh," I said, mentally struggling to understand why he was linking the Democrats' donkey to the Republicans.

"They will hound that family into doing things that will create unnecessary pain."

"Babaji, are you a Democrat?" I was puzzled to get political commentary from him. It sounded as if he didn't like the Republicans.

"I like the Democrats. They are governed by the Elephant God, Ganesha... the remover of obstacles. I am always for the people, in whatever form. The Elephant is happy, but the Jackass is stubborn, is it not?"

"They don't worship the elephant. It is just a symbol. And besides, you have it backwards. The donkey is for the Democrats, the elephant belongs to the Republicans."

"Tch!" He made the classic waggle of the head, and looked straight into my eyes with a glint of merriment. I realized he was rearranging facts to trigger my memory of this interchange.

"Symbols tell many things," Babaji hinted. "In the old days, the people supported the Rajah. He ruled for life. In your country your Emperor comes and goes too quickly."

"How to pick a good president?" I asked.

"Choose the one who likes trees and elephants. Best is to elect a woman."

"Anything more you can say?" I asked, sounding to my surprise like a political reporter.

"One word to the wise is sufficient."

Each word and gesture from Babaji was planting information inside my mind. I sensed that some was being buried for future retrieval. I intuitively knew it would bloom, like buds in springtime, when the season was at hand.

"Breathe," Babaji urged. "Make the belly soft. Strength comes from soft. When the belly is soft, then *prana* can come in."

I inhaled deeply. The white light moved down my spine.

"What exactly is *prana*, Babaji?" I asked. I wanted to know from the expert.

"*Kundalini*, *prana*, God, spiritual energy... all same. When *prana* is low, troubles come. *Prana* high, God comes. Inner Breathing fills you with prana."

I was swooning again in ecstasy as the white and golden lights circulated.

"What are the lights?"

"You are seeing the lights of *Kundalini shakti*," Babaji answered. "Spiritual growth happens when *Kundalini* awakens. Sincere Inner Breathing automatically awakens *Kundalini*. Regular practice keeps *Kundalini* awakened."

"How many times should one do this breathing?"

"Seven breaths once a day...with concentration. This is powerful meditation breath."

"That's *all*?" I asked. This seemed easy enough for anyone.

"Yes, Americans are too busy for long meditations."

"Can they do more?" I asked.

"Yes, of course...if desired. But don't do more Inner Breathing."

"What do they do more of?" I wondered.

Babaji was still rocking back and forth. He answered my silent question.

"For twenty minutes bring balance to the breath. Inhalation, retention, exhalation...all same. Same duration. Balanced breath, balanced mind, balanced life. Unbalanced breath, unbalanced life."

My own breathing started to become balanced as he spoke.

"Does Greg like to play golf?" Babaji asked about Marilyn's oldest son.

"Yes," I said.

"Golf is a good time to breathe. There are many trees."

How did Babaji know about golf? I always considered it somewhat a waste of time.

"It is not a waste of time," he answered my mental comment. "Golf is like meditation. Much concentration, breathing. Inner Breathing will help golfers. It is good for all sports. Golf is good. It is good that America has sports. These games build body and character."

I wouldn't be seeing golf again in quite the same way.

"The *Kundalini* likes play. Life is a game to be played. Sports remind us of the Play of Life. Art and music are also sports. The *shakti* likes it when we play. Krishna plays. This divine play is called *leela*. When we have no *leela*, life can appear dull. The spiritual energies stagnate. There is not enough play in the American people. Their spirits are suffering from too much work. There is too much focus on the material and not enough on the spiritual...play is spiritual."

He crossed his right leg over his left and bounced his bare foot up and down.

"Marilyn likes to play. She is *leela*." He stated it as fact. There was no doubt in my mind that eventually Marilyn would have a new name.

"Babaji, she is constantly working for others. She works seven days a week. Normally, I see her putting in fifteen to eighteen hours a day on her projects."

"Yes, yes. She loves her readers and it is also the old karma working itself out. It will work out faster through play. She is trying to win the love of her parents. She has the working habit...but soon she will develop the *leela* habit as well. What is white can become black, and what is black can become white. Such are Babaji's ways. Marilyn will show many how to play. The *leela* of laughter, song, dance and play is essential to spiritual growth and happiness. The *Kundalini* awakens to play just as a child is excited by the sight of toys."

I was trying to absorb everything that Babaji was saying. *Dhyana Loka*, this plane of alternative reality, took some getting used to. I was struggling to remember every word.

"Much of this will be hidden. My words will return to you at the appropriate time. Your body will undergo some changes that will take a little longer than one year. I am remaking your nervous system so that it can more readily radiate my blessing energy. Thoughts can change in an instant, but the body is matter and takes more time."

I was floating in a pool of warm golden light. I could hear Babaji's words, but I couldn't see him.

"When the year is up, you will be wanting to have more fresh foods. Many days you will eat only fresh fruits. On other days you will take only water. I control these days. You won't remember the words, but the process will happen naturally. It is an unfolding."

His slender body came back into focus upon the swing. His face was one big smile.

"Why fruits, Babaji?

"Fruits are divine food. They bring sweetness to the body and to the mind. When you eat fruit you are happy, because the *kundalini* likes sweets."

I recalled that Babaji was essentially a *breatharian*, a person who subsists upon air rather than food. In the 1930s a Catholic saint, Mother Theresa Neuman, was studied by medical doctors for her ability to subsist without food for more than forty years. Each day she took only one communion host, and one ounce of water. Truly we don't live by just bread alone.

"As you grow spiritually, you change your diet. Before you begin, you choose meat and a mixed diet. This brings much suffering. Then you evolve, and you choose foods that are acquired with less violence to life. At this stage you become a vegetarian. Some remain at this level. Others choose to evolve and select only fresh fruits and perhaps a little dairy. These are the fruitarians. After some time on this stage, a few will become pure breatharians...existing exclusively upon the Inner Breath. Each stage brings great health rewards, but the transition to a lighter diet must be done gradually and sensibly."

"Must Americans give up their hamburgers?" I asked. I clearly couldn't see the average American giving up the ubiquitous bacon and cheeseburger to become more spiritual.

"No. It is not an artificial game built around the desire of the ego to be spiritual. If one practices the Inner Breathing regularly, the body will begin to indicate its preferences. The process is gentle, and it varies from person to person. For some, the process may take several lifetimes. For others, it may take many years. One can't abuse the body to make progress. These things happen naturally. Vegetarianism is a special way of life. It requires special preparation to live this way intelligently...but properly followed, it brings health."

"How does one start?"

"Make no sudden changes. Let go of coffee, cigarettes and alcohol. Begin the practice of Inner Breathing. This is enough for many months. This alone will bring more peace into one's life. Every food and drink you take will be from my divine suggestion. It will be transformed into *prana* whatsoever it is."

"Mr. Donald, sir, some coconut water, sir." It was Babu, who was shaking me. I was lying face down upon the ground, my head buried in the lotus petals beneath the Shiva statue.

How did I leave my meditative posture? How long had I been lying there? I must have been "asleep" for hours. I quickly glanced at my watch. It was 11:11 A.M. My journey into the alternative reality had lasted approximately ten minutes.

Babu was handing me a green coconut with a straw in it.

"Drink."

My body was thirsty and I quickly drank the sweet coconut water. Babu was dusting some dirt off of my shirt.

"Did you have a good meditation?" he asked.

"Yes."

The memory of what happened was fading away. I could only recall a sense of happiness and inner warmth.

"We go now to Kerala? I take you to a Jewish temple. There is powerful rabbi there."

"Is the temple far?" I asked.

"Only one, two hours, most, sir," Babu answered.

We were off to Kerala.

Babu and I sailed smoothly out of Bangalore, but not more than five miles down the road we encountered a massive traffic jam that lasted for six hours. Apparently the one-lane artery out of the city was being repaired, and the work was causing major delays. We probably averaged about one mile per hour. Many stranded truckers climbed out of their cabs and slept underneath their trucks, where they could find some shade and some relief from the sun. The roadwork delays were only aggravated by drivers who stopped in the road and left their trucks to answer the call of nature.

I stayed with the Ambassador and did my best to get comfortable. The heat was stifling. An enterprising young man, barefoot and clad only in faded green shorts, worked his way down the line, offering to wash windshields for a few rupees. He wiped the countless windows—cars, buses, trucks—with the same dirty cloth.

We were trapped in a long, low ravine, hemmed in on both sides by mountains of red clay. There was little vegetation. As far as the eye could see in front and behind, was a solid stream of idling vehicles, mostly over-sized trucks spewing their ghastly black poisons into the air. There were no gas stations or stores—no restrooms and nowhere to buy some water. We couldn't turn around and backtrack to town because the one-lane road was completely clogged with vehicles. Nobody could move. We would occasionally inch forward, sometimes waiting an hour between brief moments of progress. I left the windows rolled down and sat motionless. I knew any movement would only increase my body temperature and my thirst.

Babu periodically left the car to join some of the truckers in their cabs. For these professional drivers, the delay was a normal disruption. They were happy napping, resting and taking the opportunity to socialize. What amazed me most was the fact that despite the heat and congestion I heard no angry honking of horns or frustrated outbursts or exchanges. None. Nobody was impatient.

Late that night, Babu dropped me off at a small three-story hotel in a tiny village not far off the main road. He planned to sleep in the car. A "porter," who also filled the roles of night clerk and housekeeper, carried my suitcase and led me to my room, which proved to be tiny.

There was a single bed with a foam mattress and no pillow. The mattress was covered with a single thin white sheet striped with black grease marks. There was no toilet in the room. Guests shared an Indian-style hole-in-the-floor down the hall. My room had a small drain in the floor and a bucket. The porter took the bucket and explained that he would return it in the morning with hot water so I could "shower." There was a small sink near the drain, but when I turned the handles no water came out. Above the sink, a clouded shaving mirror was haphazardly glued to the wall.

I sat on the bed and performed the Inner Breathing. After one or two repetitions I was asleep. The next thing I heard was a knock on the door at 6:00 A.M. As I awoke I felt an unbearable itching all over my feet. They were completely covered with mosquito bites.

I opened the door to discover the bucket of hot water that had been promised to me the night before. I bathed, dressed in my teddy bear uniform, and an hour later was outside, ready to proceed on our journey to the temple.

But the Ambassador was gone and there was no sign of Babu. Why hadn't we agreed on a departure time? The sun was rising and it was already hot. India was coming alive and the road would soon be teeming with activity. I had no idea where Babu was, or if he would even return, and was gripped with fear that I might be stranded in this tiny primitive village in the middle of nowhere.

At the front desk, I checked with the clerk.

"Babu taxi?" I said hopefully.

The man looked at me blankly. He spoke no English.

"Babu taxi?" I repeated, making a steering gesture with my hands. Again a blank stare.

"Babu here, sir." Babu's voice came from behind me. "We go to temple?"

I was enormously relieved to see him. His white clothes were fresh and looked neatly pressed. When my luggage was taken from the trunk the night before, I had seen only a spare tire, a tire iron and a soiled green rag—no sign of an overnight bag for Babu. How had he managed to stay clean-shaven and cleanly dressed? It was a mystery to me.

A fresh stick of Shiva incense was filling the cab with its aroma. The smoke drifted gently upward, then lazily snaked along the roof and out the windows.

"Flowers for you, Swamiji." Babu placed a fresh garland of jasmine around my neck. The sweet fragrance reminded me of Babaji.

"We go to Cochi today?" Babu asked. Although the city is called Cochin on the map, Babu and the locals called it Cochi, an affectionate term.

"Cochi? I thought we were going to the temple in Kerala?"

"Yes, sir. Cochi is the city in Kerala where we find the temple."

"Is it far?"

"Not more than one or two hours, sir."

We had trouble getting out of the village. Apparently, there had been an intense election campaign and someone had set fire to a bank on the main street (a dirt road). It had spread to nearby buildings, and several businesses had been destroyed. A riot ensued, and the army had rushed in to maintain order. We were forced to take a long, winding detour around the village. There was no road—we drove on open dirt. After what seemed painfully slow progress, I realized we'd circled the village three times. The police were merely directing everyone around and around the village.

A few hours later, we finally entered the state of Kerala, and I saw beauty like none other I'd seen in India. Gentle emerald-green hills rolled up against a backdrop of purple and green mountains, jagged against the clear blue sky, which was dotted with wispy puffs of clouds. The soil was an incredible orange-brown, and seemed to be rich, judging by the agriculture that flourished everywhere. I saw rice paddies and fields of cabbabe. Boys herded pigs and goats across the road and we frequently had to stop. Cows grazed on the side of the road, the bells around their necks clanking as they lumbered in syncopation with the occasional crack of the cowherd's whip—a simple rope and stick.

Crews of men and women, slender and resplendent in *lunghis* and colorful *saris*, tossed rice from huge flat woven baskets into the air to separate the grain from the chaff and the husks. The sunshine reflected brilliantly along the river, where women in saris of vivid hues washed clothes noisily, slapping them on the rocks. Men in loincloths bathed among naked frolicking children, who played in the water and swam. This was a scene of happy, robust people, and I noticed the absence of the Americanization that I'd seen further in the North. There were no billboards, no neon ads for beer or cigarettes; just an ancient, gentle rhythm of life. Everywhere bright-eyed children squealed in delight. Kerala is beautiful. It was the greenest, lushest part of India that I'd seen.

"My family is from Cochi, sir."

"You are lucky that you had the good fortune to live in this part of the country."

"Yes, we have been here for many generations. Only just recently have some family moved away. The Muslims don't like the Jews, sir. Now our community is less than a hundred people."

"Less than a hundred Jews in Cochin? How many *were* there?"

"Our people settled in Cochi during King Solomon's reign. We were part of the Lost Tribes. We were once thousands."

We wound our way through the back streets of Cochin to a quiet suburb called Cragnalore. Finally we came to a little sign with an arrow and both Hindu and English writing: "Jew Town Road."

"Dr. Donald, sir, you meet with the rabbi. He gives the blessing."

I tried to picture an Indian rabbi giving a blessing.

"He's got the magic, sir. If you have any difficulty at all, he touches, and pain is gone."

We finally arrived at the Pardesi Synagogue. Inside were bookshelves holding several ancient-looking scrolls in silver cylinders, which I took to be Torahs. Babu spoke Hindi to some of the temple caretakers. I waited by the door with my sandals off. Crows gathered on a nearby building. Two thin, short-haired blond puppies chased each others' tails.

"He's coming, sir." It was Babu. He sounded excited and gratified that he was successfully making this meeting happen.

Although I hadn't planned on coming to India to meet a rabbi, I was very happy with this opportunity. I felt Babaji's flow. Just a few days earlier, I had been promoting a book in Australia. In my wildest dreams I couldn't have imagined then that I'd soon be standing outside a Jewish temple in Cochin, waiting for a rabbi.

A thin Indian man approached. He looked young enough to be Babu's son, and was similarly dressed in neatly pressed white shirt and pants. He had short dark hair, but his paies, his sideburns, were long and curly. The word "pious" in English comes from the Hebrew word for sideburns. My eyes rested on the silver Star of David around his neck.

"I'm Nathan. I'm the rabbi," he said in perfect Brooklyn English. He took my hand and pumped it up and down vigorously. I felt awkward when he failed to let it go, but this soon passed as his jolly nature and sparkling eyes captivated me. There was something about him that was immediately lovable and sincere.

"You don't look like a rabbi," I said, my hand still in his.

"You don't look like a swamy," he said jokingly. His joviality made everything he said sound like it was setting up for a punch line. I had the impulse to laugh.

"Swamy?" I was onto Babaji's *leela*. "So, you were sent to me by Babaji?" I asked. At that moment, I felt Babaji was connected to everyone I was meeting.

"Who?" Nathan asked, with a puzzled look.

"Babaji."

"Never heard of him."

"Then why did you call me swamy?" I asked.

"Babu, your driver, told me you were a swamy. Besides you look like one."

The teddy bear is apparently a potent icon, I thought to myself, and said, "Well, I think I'm in the process of becoming a swamy." His good humor was contagious.

"Are you really a rabbi?" I asked, half in jest.

"I was ordained in Manhattan," he said matter-of-factly.

"Then, you are a long way from home," I stated.

"New York is wonderful, but India is my home. I serve many Jews throughout India, but I completed my studies to become a rabbi in your country. Swamys wander, but I am a wandering rabbi."

Flashing white teeth, Nathan's smile kept up the comical tension. Like Billy Crystal or Robin Williams, just the way he said things made me want to laugh. He embodied the playful aspect of the spiritual nature. He was able to pull laughter from those around him. His hands were constantly moving. Every word was punctuated by a gesture.

"Babu tells me you have the magic."

"I wonder what he meant by that?" Nathan raised his eyebrows and looked puzzled again.

"He said that you bless people and they heal?" I nudged him, hoping for an insight.

"Oy-Vey! It's annoying is what it is." He slapped the sides of his head with his palms, belying the obvious truth with his modesty.

"Why is it annoying?" I asked, noticing that more crows were gathering across the street from the temple. There were at least a dozen or so. One flew to the ground and walked toward us. It seemed to swagger and move with a belligerent attitude. When it was about twenty feet away it stopped, as if it had encountered an invisible wall. Its shiny black eyes were sinister. In a nearby tree, I saw an alarmed monkey scoop up the smallest of her three children. Scampering down the tree, she led her brood away from the crows, and over to the temple. They clambered skillfully up the walls to the roof. The mother turned and looked back at the crows, jutting her chin out and baring her teeth.

"I have to keep moving around like that mama monkey... otherwise the crowds that gather become too much for me to handle. There is so much pain and suffering in India. I have to leave about every two or three days. It's annoying, like I said." He shrugged his thin shoulders, and rubbed his hands together as if he were washing them with soap.

"Did they teach you to heal as a rabbi?"

"Do rabbis know about these things?" he asked me. "This wasn't something I learned in school. They can't teach you this. It's a gift. It came to me after I returned to India."

"How did it happen?" I yearned to understand.

"I was meditating one morning."

"I didn't know that rabbis meditate," I said, forgetting in that moment the rich tradition of mystical *Rebbes* such as the famous Bal Shem Tov.

"Of course! It's a practice from the *Kabalah*. I quiet my mind and slow my breathing so that I can become Hashem's messenger."

"Hashem," I repeated the word softly, and felt spiritually energized by divine contact through the name.

"It is an orthodox way to say God."

"So you heal through the power of Hashem?" I asked. I realized I was thirsty, but ignored it, spellbound by Nathan.

"No, you're going to think this is strange. I got this power from an old Jewish woman. She came to me in meditation.

She's what you might call an angel."

He studied my face for my reaction. I nodded to indicate that he should go on.

"I can't tell you much more. She came to me in my meditation and said she was here to help heal families, the mothers and the children. Her name is Elie." At the mention of the name Elie, the entire congregation of crows let out a raucous cackle.

"Those crows give me the creeps," I said. A cold chill surged through my body.

"Of course they do. Some of them are the eyes and ears of the Dark Lord," he said in a whisper.

"The Dark Lord?"

"Ahriman...Set...Beelzebub...Satan. When evil spirits die, some take animal forms to serve Satan. The enemies of good are everywhere."

He glanced somewhat defiantly toward the crows, as if he were openly confronting evil. I watched the crows gather around their leader.

"We are either serving the God of Good or the God of Evil. Every day, every moment, we've got to make the choice. Life is a continual struggle between good and evil, isn't it?"

I nodded agreement.

"I've got to get about my business," he said cheerfully, a happy representative of the Good. "Elie and I have some people to heal. Want to come along?"

We walked about a mile down a narrow road lined with primitive dwellings to a rustic-looking Indian hut. Before us was a line of at least a hundred people waiting to see the rabbi. One man without legs dragged himself along the ground with his arms. The woman behind him was covered with hideous scales...a leper. A father carried a dead infant while the mother wailed beside him. The crows had followed us.

They were perched in a tree above the suffering, and cackled in a way that resembled laughter.

The rabbi sat down and began to meditate. The crowd hushed and waited. "Elie . . . Elie . . . Elie," I heard him say in a low, musical whisper.

I suddenly had goose bumps, and when he pronounced the name for the third time, I felt bathed by something clean and luminous, as if the purity of this "angel" was an energy washing over me.

"*What?*" he then said, in a tone that conveyed amazement. He lowered his voice and was talking to himself, but I couldn't hear the words. Many in the crowd were bowing to him at this time.

"He's getting the magic now, sir." It was Babu. Babu sat down behind me and began softly chanting.

"Om Namah Shivaya, Om Namah Shivaya, Om Namah Shivaya."

"I use this chant to Shiva to ward off evil, sir," Babu suddenly paused to explain. "It means, 'I honor God in the form of Shiva.'"

Nathan raised his hands in the air as if he were gathering some invisible manna from heaven. Then he clapped his hands together in prayer and opened his eyes. He turned toward me.

"Elie says you know her . . . that you helped her when she was living."

"I've never known an Elie my entire life," I said.

"It's not possible. Elie's never wrong. Search your mind," Nathan demanded.

"I don't know an Elie," I replied.

"You *do* know her."

I shrugged my shoulders. I couldn't recall ever meeting an Elie.

"Elie works with you. She watches over you and your wife and family. She told me." His look said it couldn't be any other way.

"Maybe. Who knows," I said. I didn't want to argue with Nathan or Elie, whoever she was.

"Elie says that you carry a magic stone. She has one too. She says you can use it for healing. She wants you to help us today with *your* magic."

"I don't have a magic stone," I said.

"Dr. Donald, sir, you have crystal stone. I saw it at the Shiva temple. You gave blessing to the woman," Babu said.

"Oh…right!" I didn't think of the Shiva power object from Babaji as a "stone." I made a mental note to be more discreet with it. Babaji had commanded me not to show it to anyone.

"I can't let anyone see it. Perhaps I can hold it in my hand and touch some people?" People were still streaming into the area, and the crowd had doubled in size. This street of humble dwellings was filled with people.

"Yes, Swamiji, that would be fine. I'm happy you're here. See, Elie is right. This is a special day." He said something to the people in the local dialect. Many turned and bowed in my direction. I returned the bow. I felt awkwardly on display.

"Elie is letting me rest today!" Nathan looked relieved.

I had no idea who "Elie" was, but I was intrigued by the reference to the stone. It pulsated within my shirt pocket. I took it out and held it tightly within my left fist.

The people approached, slowly at first. I touched each one on the top of the head with the Shiva crystal. Each person was grateful, but nothing seemed to be happening.

"Tch! Go into your heart!" It was the voice of Babaji. "Don't concentrate on the outer...it is illusion, *maya.* Go to the truth of the *inner* reality...all is perfect...see and know the perfection...see the perfect condition of each person...more importantly...*Feel it.*"

"You tell him, Babaji!" It was the voice of an elderly woman. Was this Elie? She sounded strangely familiar.

I felt a powerful current...actually an electric shock go through the left side of my body from my head to my toes, and was aware of the pleasing smell of apple pie and chicken soup. As I was fasting, it brought up a tremendous longing for food.

"For your soul...a little apple pie and some chicken soup," Elie said. "How can a man work without food in his stomach?"

I felt instantly full as if I'd had a meal. I could actually taste apple pie—even the crust. Visions of large golden-crusted pies danced before me. And I was also no longer thirsty.

"This one is all in his head." It was Elie. Was she talking to Babaji? "Now that his stomach is full he can go into his heart."

I didn't have any more time to speculate because the woman with leprosy was now before me. Her tormented brown eyes were downcast and solemn. I placed my left hand upon her head. The Shiva crystal pulsated in three quick distinct beats. After the third beat, the woman began to shriek and hop around on one foot, convulsing, as if her feet were on fire.

Nathan rose quickly and was standing beside me.

"She's got a devil in her!" he exclaimed.

The young woman let out an ear-piercing scream and fell backward to the ground. The crowd backed away and all eyes were upon her as she rolled around in the dirt, wailing piteously. A solitary crow swooped down and buzzed her body, nearly touching her, then flew upwards and circled above. The woman lay curled up in fetal position, groaning as a black shadowy form, a cloud-like vapor, rose out of her body. It continued to rise, until it seemed to surround and enter the crow. The crow flapped its wings vigorously and disappeared.

"Look! Swamiji! She is healed!" Babu was pointing to the young woman, who was now being lifted up by Nathan and some members of the crowd. Her skin was remarkably restored, smooth and shiny like a newborn's, without a blemish. I was learning, and would continue to learn, that spiritual power has no limits.

I will always stand in awe of the miracles that flow from Babaji's hands through me. In the months ahead, through his grace, I would see many similar miracles, as others received the healing touch. Cripples would be carried toward me, and walk away under their own power. I would see twisted bones straighten under my hand. Terrible cancer would vanish, scheduled back surgery would be unnecessary, and hearts would mysteriously repair.

Not everyone who came would receive a miracle healing, at least not instantly. Working on matter takes time, and for many, lifestyle changes would also be necessary. I believed they all received some benefit, but faith and karma probably played roles in the extent. Such miracles must be experienced firsthand to be fully grasped. Even still, there will always be critics who negate the triumph of spirit over matter. Spiritual literature is rich with miraculous stories of healings that took place around Buddha, Mohammed, Jesus Christ and many others.

Miracles happened around Nathan. There is a tradition of healing rabbis from Lithuania, Poland and Russia about whom stories of miracles are often recounted.

The healing of the woman with leprosy caused the crowd to surge ahead with excitement. People pushed forward and surrounded me. A sea of hands reached out to touch me. I feared I would suffocate within the press of bodies, and the pressure kept increasing. For fifteen minutes, I did my best to help the people in front of me, but I was becoming hot and claustrophobic. I wanted to keep helping, but I was overwhelmed. I couldn't see Nathan or Babu. I felt like one of the Beatles in *A Hard Day's Night*. The real possibility of being trampled to death was right in front of me.

A horn blared.

"Here, sir!" I faintly heard Babu and saw him waving frantically in the Ambassador, yelling from the street. Nathan was helping the crowd make way for me as I struggled toward the car and climbed in. Once the door was shut, Nathan leaned in over me, the crowd still pressing behind him.

"This is the work I do every day," he said, his voice nearly drowned out by the clamor behind him. "This is why I continuously move around India. Elie's power is tremendous, but the crowds become unruly... like I said, *annoying*!" Nathan smiled.

"Thank you for this opportunity, Nathan," I said.

"When I became a rabbi I took a vow to serve the people. I long ago tired of earthly pleasures. This is my joy. My duty. This is all we can do for God. *Shalom*, my brother."

He said *Shalom*, while bowing *Namaste* fashion. The way he pronounced the word emphasized the *Om. Shal-Om.*

"*Shalom*," I returned. *Shalom* and *Namaste* are similar in meaning. Both mean "Peace and God are within you."

Babaji had told me that there would be much I wouldn't remember, that my mystical experiences would be concealed until the right moment for the veils of *Maya* to be lifted. I had already lost much of the detail of my time with him, and my experience with Nathan was immediately shrouded. I did not recollect it for over a year. Like a child, who is born with total recall of the angelic realms, but loses it gradually over the first few years of life, as Babaji's newborn I was losing memory of his physical presence in my life.

The car slowly pulled away from the crowd in Cochi.

"We go to Tiruvannamali, sir?" Babu asked, lighting a fresh stick of Shiva incense with one hand. His good-natured manner reflected the Hindu "another day in India, we've-seen-it-all" psychology. Rabbi Nathan was still waving, and so was the crowd. I reached out the window and waved back.

"Is Tiruvannamali far from here?" I was afraid of the answer, so I supplied it. "I bet it is only one or two hours away, Babu."

"No sir, it will take us a full day! Maybe a day and a half. It *is* far, sir!" He chuckled.

I settled Buddha-like into the back of the cab. *Premananda* was calling.

The experience of being fully present in the here and now was opening up for me. My mind wandered less and less to my past or to my imagined future. As I became fully aware of the present moment, I was in the alternative reality. More and more, a sense of harmony, quiet and light surrounded each moment.

"Where am I?" I often wondered during this period. Babaji's voice frequently responded from within: "You are home."

I couldn't even define the concept of home anymore, at least not in terms of a physical location. Home was a feeling I carried inside myself. The people I saw were no longer "them." It was all just us. There was no distance between me and anyone else. I was in a state of unity where we all are, all the time, if we are aware of it.

I was truly practicing living life in the present, and witnessing how the mind can drag us out of it. So I would ask myself, "Are you thinking about the rabbi again? Are you mentally anticipating the next stop in Tiruvannamali?" As I rode in the taxi, hour after hour, I continued to return my awareness more fully to the present moment, not focusing on anything in particular, just allowing it to be in the here and now. Whenever I did, Babaji was fully present.

From this perspective the car and Babu were merely illusions. We were, in fact, going nowhere, because there was nowhere to go. Yet, my journey in the outer world triggered experiences in my inner world. Both worlds exist simultaneously. It was only a matter of which one I "tuned" into.

And the geography of the inner world was beckoning more strongly than that of the outer world. Inward was the mystery of the Self. In the outside world I experienced the unfolding of Babaji's will, each and every moment. Babaji arrives into each new moment when we are fully present, or rather, he is "here" all the time as we discover him. The place within me that was watching the drama of life unfold was Babaji. He had always been observing my life, like a helicopter hovering above rush hour, reporting on the traffic. The realization that he was more aware of me than I could ever be was one of the last thoughts my old self entertained.

"Acha! You are not your mind and body. Babaji change the old. To become a swamy means the old self dies. All is Babaji's *sankalpa* (will). When the petals of the lotus bloom, it is Babaji's *sankalpa.* There is no longer ego in you. There is nobody home. Only the Self exists. You are no longer alive to the world. You belong to the Self. Others will see only the matter of clay. All is *leela.* Tch."

I don't know how much time had passed when I heard, "Swamy, we are here." It was Babu. He opened his door and exited the Ambassador, stretched and yawned. He was clean-shaven and his clothing was still immaculate, right down to the creases in his pants.

We were parked in front of the ashram of the famous yogic sage, Ramana Maharshi, in the lovely town of Tiruvannamali, in the tropical Indian jungle. The ashram was inside a fenced compound, nestled in foothills at the base of Arunachala Mountain, which rose in the distance. The atmosphere was charged and quieting at the same time. My eyes took in trees full of crows—more crows than I'd ever seen; perhaps two hundred. Beggars lined the outside of the ashram, or temple. Many approached the car and asked for rupees. Babu did his best to chase them away.

"Professional beggars, sir. They hang around the shrines waiting for foreign tourists to prey upon."

As I drew closer to the holy shrine of the master, I found myself involuntarily closing my eyes frequently and breathing deep Inner Breaths. I consciously affirmed my connection to Babaji and his *prana*, and felt my oneness with all.

Near the ashram bookstore I was greeted by an Indian swamy in an orange lunghi. Draped around his shoulders was a plain yellow shawl, which he used to cover his head from the sun.

"*Namaste*!" he said. He was middle-aged, with a clean-shaven head and small wire glasses. He had a quiet demeanor and radiated a no-nonsense attitude: a true ascetic.

"*Namaste*!" I returned. Many buses had stopped outside the compound, and the crowd of temple visitors was rapidly swelling. Devout Indians of all persuasions knew that Ramana Maharshi was a great saint. Just as Americans would stop to see the Lincoln Memorial or the Statue of Liberty, Indians frequented this place. The ashram was also one of the few places in town to find warm food and a restroom.

Somehow, the swamy sensed I was not one of the typical tourists stopping merely for coffee or tea. Nor was I the average foreign seeker, looking only to purchase flowers or candy, or take some snapshots of the quaint village. He led me away from the crowd, some distance behind the ashram, where we proceeded to mount a difficult path up Arunachala Mountain, where Ramana Maharshi had often sat in meditation.

While he was alive, seekers traveled from every corner of the world for the opportunity to sit in the presence of this spiritual giant. The "Guru of Woodstock," Swamy Satchidananda; the writer, Thomas Mann; and that icon of Eastern spiritual literature, Paul Brunton, had all made pilgrimages here.

My swamy guide was taking me on this hike to accord me an unusual privilege I will always cherish. We came to a resting place, where he invited me to sit on the very spot—the hallowed earth—where the Guru Ramana Maharshi sat for long hours during his daily meditations. In this place, the vibrations of the Eternal Mother rocking her child were powerfully soothing. I could only shut my eyes and weep. Waves of God consciousness melted all physical boundaries, and there was nothing that I could sense, taste or feel but the sublime golden light. I experienced my "I" to be this golden light, an inner fire that burns but never consumes. Perhaps this was similar to what Moses encountered on Mt. Sinai when he saw the burning bush that proclaimed itself to be the "I Am."

Aha! My mission in life became crystal clear. I would be the vehicle through which Babaji would bring others to this alternative reality. Through me, they would experience the inner geography of profound tranquility that is the "personality" of the soul. It would be my mission to lead others to the realization of this state; *the truth of their own being.*

This truth is manifested as an inner light, far brighter than any outer light. This light is the only thing that is real. It is the pure, eternal light of the Self. The entire world takes birth in this light. Time and space don't exist there. It is the timeless moment.

In 1950 Ramana Maharshi's soul chose to exit his body by manifesting bone cancer. His disciples gathered around him during his final days and wept. They beseeched him to heal himself, and pleaded with him not to leave them.

"And where can "I" go?" he responded. These were his last spoken words. Indeed where can the immortal soul, what is real, ever "go"? Death is a fiction. It is only the body—what is transient—that leaves us like a suit of old clothes.

In deep meditation, in the vibration of the master, I experienced the living omnipresence of his soul...along with the souls of all the great masters. This was Babaji's *Premananda*, the land of love and bliss where great beings congregate. *Prema* is Sanskrit for love, and *ananda* is Sanskrit for bliss. Images of rabbis and a brief glimpse of Mohammed filled my inner realm. Within *Premananda*, I saw mosques, temples, ashrams and churches. All represented the expressions, from the heartbeat of humanity of the one God with many names.

Hours passed like minutes. I had no idea how long I'd been there when the swamy of the temple returned. My face, neck and forearms were badly sunburned. The swamy placed a fresh garland of white flowers around my neck, and offered me a green coconut to drink.

"This is sacred place," he confided. "I sleep here at night. Please keep location secret. No one ever here before you. The moment I saw you I knew you were supposed to come here. My heart tells me you are the living one. You will carry the Master's message to the West."

"Thank you," I said quietly. I couldn't fathom anything but the now. My mind and heart were still basking in the afterglow of Babaji's *Premananda.*

We were about a mile from the temple and the shelter it offered from the blazing sun and merciless heat. I understood why only the very sincere would welcome the climb to this sacred site, but I was surprised to hear he'd brought no one there before me. I wondered why.

"The ashrams are becoming focal points for tour groups," he explained. "Vendors and thieves prey upon seekers. The money is the problem. Everybody's wanting the rupees, not the God. It is my responsibility to protect the sacred site. The money is creating tragedy." He further explained that there were other designated "official spots" used by the Master. These were easily accessible places for the tour groups or for the merely curious.

I understood the tragedy to which he was referring. In India, Western spiritual materialism had turned the holy sites into carnivals. These places, once famous for the peace they offered, now afford the sincere seeker little or nothing. They are overrun with billboards, beggars, endless soft drink concessions, and legions of traders, hawking trinkets and spiritual paraphernalia.

"Babu suggested that you spend the night in the temple. I have arranged a bed for you. You are welcome to take a meal. He will be coming for you in the morning."

An Indian horn sounded in the ashram. I recognized it to be the beginning of the evening *Arati*, a ritual chant sung before the evening meal to honor the Guru.

I wasn't at all hungry. But I was looking forward to a good night's sleep. Babaji was at work, and the veil was becoming thicker. The weeks that followed were a magical mystery tour, memory of which has not yet risen to the surface.

INITIATION

It was Christmas Eve. My whole body was singing in the joyous anticipation of being with Swamy Nagananda once again. Babu and I were like father and son. We had spent the last three weeks together, traveling around India.

"We are almost there, Babu," I said.

"Very good, sir. Is it far?" he asked with a grin, as we approached the village of my Guru. We enjoyed playing the time game together.

"No, Babu, just a few minutes."

I took in the entire scene as we approached Sri Sri Swamy Nagananda's ashram. The surrounding region reminded me of the desert and mountains of Ajo, my childhood home. It was all so familiar.

When we arrived I was greeted by Dayananda, a female swamy from Australia; Paolo, a young medical doctor from Brazil; and a physician from London named Patrick. Swamy wanted me to stay in the "wedding suite," a place that he had designed and built for the devotees who would be married in his ashram. Marilyn and I had stayed there years earlier after he performed a beautiful Hindu marriage for us. The townspeople gathered, and the festivities lasted throughout the night. Nagananda kept a video of our wedding and proudly showed it to visitors.

"Swamy wants to see you in his private room," Patrick advised. "He's acting strangely; he's sending all foreign seekers away. Particularly those who are here for materializations instead of meditation."

I knocked on the door to Swamy's room.

"Yes, yes." A sense of something wonderful about to happen fluttered within me as I heard his voice.

I entered quietly. There were no lights, and the windows were covered with cloth. I peered into the darkness to where Swamy was sitting in a chair in the corner. His bright, radiant eyes were the only lights.

"Tomorrow you take the *kashi*," he said, his voice breaking the deep meditative silence of the space. The *kashi* is the long orange or ochre robe—usually of cotton—that the traditional swamy wears. He pointed to his feet, which rested on a pile of orange cloth.

"Swamy, you look so thin," I said, as I approached and bowed to touch his feet. "Are you all right?"

"Yes, yes. Fasting is for powers. I am fasting for your ceremony. I will give you many powers."

There was silence again, and I knelt, watching him, happier than ever to be in his presence.

"You are always happy," he said. Then he gave me a teaching that would shape my life.

"Christians pray, Moslems pray, Hindus pray, Buddhists pray...but today there are few miracles. Like Gandhi, like Jesus, it is necessary to fast and pray...then at that time miracles happen. Fasting for most people not recommended beyond one to three days. There can be no ego about it. For you it is different. You not like other people. Sometimes you will fast, I will bring it to your body. No need to worry if one day, one week, or one month...Swamy will protect...just let the body fast, and know that I am working with you...but I will also be with you when you are eating. Just let things happen...simply allow."

He stopped and breathed, and I began the Inner Breathing. My whole body was listening.

"Sometimes you will feel like being lazy; then be lazy. This is what God wants you to do in that moment. Every moment is God's...stay in the moment. Sometimes you will feel so full of energy, and will want to do many things. When this happens, do many things and enjoy it. Let your energy come. Let things come easily; doing or not doing not important.

"Sometimes you will sit to meditate. If this happens then enjoy the quiet. Most importantly be *here*. Listen to each moment. Trust your energy. Go with your energy. Energy is *Kali*, the Divine Mother.[1] Let the Divine Mother be the Doer. Come closer, let me check your energy."

Swamy motioned for me to come closer and sit at his feet. He placed his fingers on the top of my head. He looked pleased.

"You are full of Mother Kali already! This is good. Take these *kashi*. Spend one hour in your room, then return to see me. Keep quiet. Quiet is meditation." Swamy handed me the orange *kashi* that had been beneath his feet. When I took them tenderly in my hands, my mind stopped. The powerful energy they had absorbed from him flooded my entire being. Quiet. Calm. Peace.

Paolo guided me to my room. More correctly, he guided the shell that was my body; there was such tranquility.

The wedding suite was a two-room apartment, built through the financial contributions of Patrick, a strong and sincere seeker who receives joy from seeing others happy. The room was quite fancy for this region of the world. There was a single cot, and a separate bathroom with a mirror, sink, Indian-style toilet, and an inoperative shower covered with spider webs. The total space of the room was probably a thousand square feet, which was quite large for an ashram room. It seemed palatial.

"Donald, I'd like to ask you about prayer." It was Paolo, hesitating at the door, obviously not wanting to leave. "I've asked swamy, but he says to ask you. I feel uncomfortable calling you Donald. Do you mind if I call you Swamiji?"

I nodded, placing the orange *kashi* carefully on a little metal folding chair. Although my Guru had instructed me to meditate, here was someone who was seeking help. Here was my first exercise in going with the energy.

Paolo's handsome face was screwed up with an inner tension. It was clear he needed to talk.

"How can I help?"

"I've been here over a month. Swamy talks about you every day. Whenever I have a spiritual question, he says to ask you. I don't want to impose, but I have a month of questions."

Paolo was wearing white cotton yoga pants and a tank top which showed his well-defined shoulder muscles. His long hair was pulled back into a ponytail.

"I'm Catholic," Paolo continued. "I started studying hatha yoga in Brazil. I wanted to learn more about meditation, so I came to India. I feel so confused. As a Catholic, I was taught to pray. Now I don't know—should I pray, or meditate? I have so many questions. I don't know why I asked you this one first, but it is important to me to know. Could you answer it... please?"

"Yes, yes," I said. "Something more?" I was beginning to sound and act like Swamy Nagananda, a process known as

GuruBhav. When you concentrate fully on your spiritual teacher his or her personality begins to come through you. The concentration must be pure and totally focused. In my inner quiet, I was still at my Guru's feet. I closed my eyes and took in a deep Inner Breath.

"I want to know about prayer," Paolo continued, "because I was taught as a child to pray. Through prayer, I was taught to give thanks to the Virgin Mother, and to Jesus. Now I don't know whom to pray to anymore. Do I pray to Swamy? Swamy says that God is just a name for one's *Atman*, the soul or inner divinity. Am I praying then to myself?" That Paolo was grappling deeply with this issue was clear from the anguish written upon his face.

I automatically took several more deep Inner Breaths. After a few minutes of silence, something within me was moved to speak.

"Prayer doesn't need to have a zip code, Paolo. In fact, the prayer that goes to a zip code is not very deep. Just let your prayer be from your heart. Don't give it an address. Let it be unaddressed."

I paused, and breathed, and my eyes closed as I was pulled involuntarily into meditation. More words bubbled up from that depth, and I opened my eyes halfway.

"Let your prayer be a song that communicates to the totality of existence, my dear Paolo." I felt his turmoil, as he looked at me intently.

"Let it reach the trees, the moon, stars and sun, the mountains, the babies. Let it reach the All. This is the meaning of God."

The look of tension had not yet left his strong chiseled jaw.

"Paolo, stop making God a person," I insisted. "God can definitely reflect in a person, but beyond any one person is the totality that even Jesus and the Mother Mary are part of. To think only of Jesus is to miss the totality, all that is, all that has been, and all that will be...even beyond all of this...lies a further shore...beyond even beyond *beyond*."

I couldn't keep my eyes open. Clearly, Swamy's directive to meditate was linked to a process I was going through with him. While the outer world of Paolo called me, the inner world pulled hard. I sought to find the balance as deeper answers came for Paolo.

"Your prayer is gratitude to the Holy One, the Whole. Learn to repeat this prayer."

I began to sing like Babaji...

Om	the sound of creation
Purnamadah	That is the Holy
Purnamidam	This is the Holy
Purnat purnamudaachyate	The Holy births the Holy
Purnasya purnamadaya	Holy comes from the Holy
Purnameva vashisyate	And Holy still remains

"Paolo, you belong to the whole. You come from the whole. You live in it, Paolo, and one day you will dissolve back into it. It is your home. Through prayer and meditation you can return to it. At the heart of this world of *maya*, or appearance, with all its changing forms, lives the unchanging God. Go beyond the changing outer world, and enjoy the inner changeless reality."

I was settled on the cot in a cross-legged position, and Paolo was sitting in front of me cross-legged on the floor. The words were still coming from *Premananda*, deep within me. My connection with that realm was more powerful than my worldly connection at that moment.

"So then," Paolo burst forth, "you are saying it is fine for me to pray?"

"Yes, yes," I agreed. "Of course!" He relaxed and I could feel his happiness.

"But don't just pray robotically," I cautioned. "*Use* prayer to remember your h-om-e, your source, your goal. It is simply a remembering. To 're-Member' means to become whole again. When you pray you remind yourself that you are not separate from the great ocean of existence."

"How do we forget that we are whole—that we are divine?" he asked.

"The very nature of the world causes us to continually forget," I said. "Spiritual life is a *sadhana.* This is a Sanskrit word that refers to the continual daily practices and activities that keep us spiritually awake. The world causes us to fall asleep, and then we use only our ego. I call 'Paolo,' and you have to answer as Paolo, with all the characteristics of your ego crystallized into the world of *maya.* Paolo is illusion, part of the *maya,* but it is a necessary, learned device that you must use to relate to other people. Prayer is an *upaya,* or method, to relax again into that feeling of non-separation with the totality. Just forget the illusion of your being separate. Take a moment here and there to "re-Member" and to connect with this alternative reality." I paused and remained quiet, my eyes closing involuntarily to shut out the world of *maya.*

"So, are you saying that prayer is a meditation?" Paolo persisted.

My heart began to ache with the inner calling of Babaji. Even though Paolo was talking to me and I was in discourse, I wanted the answers to come from *Premananda.* The quieter I became, and the more I worked with the Inner Breath, the more the wisdom from the inner realm flowed through.

"Prayer and meditation, they are the two wings of the bird, Paolo. The bird can't fly with only one wing. Prayer is *certainly* meditation. It is a form of spoken meditation, an *active* form, delivered with love. Prayer must be full of music. It is a *gita*, a song. When Krishna plays his flute, he is praying to God. Stop making it so complicated for yourself, my dear Paolo."

He looked at me, a smile playing upon his lips.

"Yeah, that's me, I've always made *everything* hard for myself."

"Well, now you can stop!" I continued. "Life is *leela*—a divine play. Let your prayers be poetic and from the heart. Learn to dance, and let your dancing be a prayer. Celebrate God with your love. If you are praying, there is no need to meditate at that moment. Prayer is action. Meditation is silence. Use them both, and soar to the heavenly heights. Sometimes pray. Sometimes meditate. Both are important. Both are good."

Paolo's face was illumined with rays of gratitude and relief. He leaned back and stretched his spine, rolled his neck from one side to the other, and grinned broadly, like a little child. Clearly, he was more relaxed. Then he stood up, came forward and hugged me.

"Thank you. You've been a great help!" He laughed, and in my quiet space, I reveled in his joy of liberation. He glanced at his watch.

"I've been instructed to return you to Swamy in an hour. We must go!" He helped me up, guiding me in my waking trance.

We walked through the trees to the temple. A young Indian assistant to Swamy told us that he was waiting for me in his private room, and I was to go in.

Swamy Nagananda was sitting on the floor. His chest was bare and he was only wearing an orange *lunghi*. He motioned for me to sit in front of him. Several minutes of silence passed.

"It is difficult for people to meditate," he began. "They must first establish control over their mind. As long as the mind wanders, the *Atman*, the Self, cannot be realized or enjoyed. This control is the greatest problem for humanity. The restless mind must be quieted. When one conquers the mind he becomes the King of Kings."

Swamy looked at me, flashing his charismatic Tyrone Power grin. His deep burnished skin and shiny blue-black hair flecked with gray were radiant in the rays of light coming in from the one small, high window.

"Some trouble?" he asked. I knew he was aware that I'd brought with me to India deep prayers for the welfare of my son and stepchildren. "Are you worried about the children? The children are fine. Swamy is with them."

I didn't feel any trouble in that moment. I was feeling quite peaceful. I'd learned that how I felt was irrelevant to Swamy's questions. He could at any moment be talking to my past self, or even a future self. It could also be that he was talking to another soul through me. Perhaps he was connecting to my son Michael, or stepchildren Greg, Lisa and Beau at that moment through me. I remained silent and open. I just listened.

"Much fighting in the world over religion. Many people react unnecessarily to words. When someone is called a fool, it doesn't make them a fool. If I call you an elephant do you grow a trunk and tail? Yet people react to words with such anger. It is a weakness of the mind. Moslems fight with Jews. Protestants fight with Christians. Everywhere on this planet people see themselves as different rather than as one. They cannot restrain the mind, so there is fighting."

"Should I teach them to suppress their minds Swamy?"

"No! Suppression is bad. It leads to madness. They must restrain their thoughts. Restraint is not the same as suppression.

When people suffer abuse, it does no good to suppress the anger. Any suppression is bad. Sadness, depression...the restrained thoughts must be given expression...but a proper expression. It is good to channel such thoughts into mantra repetition, exercise, meditation, or even thinking opposite thoughts. If you are sad, think happy thoughts. Soon you will be happy. Mantra is very powerful meditation. Mantra leads to God. You will bring a powerful mantra to the world. The Divine Mother will bring it to you."

Swamy grew silent, and I closed my eyes and listened within. Slowly, the sound of *Om-Prema-Om* came to me. Om is the infinite source of all creation. *Prema* is divine love. "*Om-Prema-Om*," I repeated inwardly.

"The mantra is the very body of God. Always treat it with respect. It is a gift from the Mother. *Japamala*[2] is good."

As he sat before me cross-legged, Swamy abruptly reached into the air with his left hand, and an uncommonly huge and beautiful *rudraksha* necklace materialized with a flash of light into his hand. The beads were colossal, a half-inch in diameter at least, and they were a deep, rich brown color. An exotic fragrance of sweet, spicy sandalwood poured into the room.

"This from Kali, the Divine Mother," he said.

Swamy abruptly reached into the air again, this time with his right hand, and an identical *rudraksha* necklace materialized into it.

"From Shiva, the Divine Father," he said.

"All powers coming now from within. *Atman* is the source of all powers. Best power is to know the *Atman*. The necklace is a symbol of the *Atman*."

He leaned forward and placed the two necklaces around my neck. The remarkable, fragrant aroma lifted me inwardly. I closed my eyes and felt myself rising higher and higher. I kept rising and rising. I saw myself sitting on Arunachala Mountain with Ramana Maharshi. Above us was Babaji sitting in his swing. Babaji lifted his hands to suggest that we go higher... higher.

"You have friends in high places," Swamy Nagananda offered.

My eyes were still closed. His words reached my heart. I was listening from my heart and not my ears. My eyes were closed and I couldn't open them. I didn't want to open them. My nostrils were filled with the blissful, ethereal scent, and it was taking me still higher and higher.

"The mountains, the trees are your friends. The Maha-Avatar is your friend... the Divine Mother is your friend. Everywhere you will be surrounded with friends," Swamy said.

I was continuing to rise, floating high above our beautiful, emerald green and royal blue planet. It is such a delicate jewel. We live on a jewel—a living, breathing jewel. She is alive. The trees are the lungs. *Mother Earth!* I finally understood. The *Om-Prema-Om* mantra permeated the air from a heavenly dimension. Babaji was still above in his swing, smiling...

"Higher," he indicated, by pointing upward beyond his head and into the blinding, radiant white-hot aura that pulsated above him.

"Swamy wants to see you soon," Paolo spoke.

I was lying on the cot in the wedding suite. Paolo was washing my feet with warm water from a green bucket. I was wearing both of the necklaces.

"They are incredible," Paolo exclaimed. "They smell heavenly."

"Swamy materialized them," I said. "How did I get here? I was with Swamy."

"Kumar, some men, and I, we carried you here from Swamy's room. You never moved a muscle. Swamy said you needed to rest. You've been here for nearly an hour." He continued to wash my feet.

"Swamiji, can I ask you another question?" He looked at me pleadingly.

I nodded, intoxicated by the indescribable aroma of the necklaces.

"As Catholics we're taught that the Pope is infallible. Is Swamy Nagananda infallible too?" Paolo was drying my feet.

"Paolo," was all I could immediately respond.

The words were coming, but slowly. I felt the automatic, rhythmic breathing of my soul.

"The enlightened ones know only themselves, and nothing more. Essentially they understand everyone, because they know themselves completely. They know how to find their inner light, and they can lead others to this light. This light is the *Atman* Swamy talks about. Knowing their true selves, they also know *your* true potential, *your* possibility.

"An enlightened one does not know the totality, couldn't know it. It is beyond the mind. This totality is the alternative reality. Our ordinary reality is included within it, like fish within the ocean. How absurd it would be for the fish to proclaim that it is the ocean, or that it knows the entire ocean. It knows only the water that flows around and through it's own body."

Paolo sat motionless before me. He seemed to be in a deep state of concentration, soaking up every word I uttered. Where were these words coming from? I had no idea what would come next. I took a deep Inner Breath.

"At one time Christianity taught that the sun revolves around the Earth. This was accepted as infallible fact. Then Galileo proved that this was just illusion, an appearance. The truth is just the opposite—the Earth revolves around the sun. Galileo published his findings and was called before the Pope.

"The Pope asked him, 'Have you written this?'

"Galileo responded, 'Yes.'

"The Pope said, 'This goes against the Bible. If you don't change it, you will be burned alive.'

"Galileo answered, 'I'm not important. You don't need to trouble yourself about me. I'm not wanting to create a problem. Of course I will change it for you. But know this, the stars, the sun and the earth will not change for Galileo.'

"Some think perhaps that Galileo was cowardly, Paolo. Should he have fought for his ideas, at the expense of his life? No. He was sane enough not to want to commit suicide. You have to admire him. He was brilliant, one of the brightest of his time. He was teaching us not to kill ourselves in the name of truth. The greatest truth is life, and life is to be cherished."

"Yeah," said Paolo, "I guess time handled the problem." We both laughed, savoring the bond we were building.

"The Bible, the Koran, the Bhagavad Gita, were all written to express truth as men and women understood it in different eras. Buddha was given a forum because he was the best representative of truth alive on the planet at that time. Moses and Jesus were respected for the same reason. Kant, Freud, Jung all had their day. Because these seekers and expounders of truth had the courage to articulate the message of sanity for their eras, we are able to grow in our wisdom and understanding, and expand upon the application of these universal truths. As we grow we can see truth more clearly, and we realize that none of them were infallible. We learn to focus on the truth rather than the individuals, on the message rather than the messengers."

I sat up and swung my legs over the edge of the cot. I suddenly wanted nothing more than to lighten Paolo's burden of seriousness around spiritual matters. I wanted to encourage him to play more at life, to celebrate his spiritual self-discovery.

"Forget about the personalities and bodies that truth may inhabit from time to time, Paolo. Go within and find your own truth. Know thyself deeply."

"Is there a method I can use to discover my own truth more quickly?" Paolo asked.

"Mantra is good for this," I answered. "Mantra is the continual repetition of a sacred word. Sacred words are imbued with power."

"Where do sacred words come from?" Paolo asked. He had scooted over, and sat near me, very straight, like a yogi.

"Sacred words are developed from sacred languages such as Hebrew, Tibetan, or Sanskrit. The letters and words are studied and meditated upon by the priests. Then they are carefully combined, and revealed to the seeker to be used to create a spiritual effect. *Shalom*, *Amen*, and *Om* are some examples," I explained.

"Can you suggest a mantra for me?" he asked.

A vibrant pause engulfed me. A multicolored glow of shimmering light filled the space between us. I was beginning to consistently find myself in this space, the alternative reality, pausing and breathing before I ever responded to a question.

"Use *Om-Prema-Om*." As I looked at Paolo, I saw him shimmering in the multicolored glow of divine light. "It means that love is the totality, the All."

"How will I use the mantra?" he asked.

"Find a quiet place. Mantras work best if you allow about 20 minutes. It takes a while for you to empty your mind of the daily chatter. If your thoughts are fast, let the mantra be fast. If your thoughts are slow, let the mantra be slow. Keep your attention on the mantra. If you think about anything else, bring your attention gently back to the mantra. Forget about the past, or the future. Just be focused in the present upon the mantra. The mantra brings you back to the present, the mantra takes you to the *now*. In the *now*, you find your soul, you find God. Let's try it."

"*Om-Prema-Om*," Paolo began.

"I'm sorry," I interrupted. "I didn't make it clear. For mantra meditation, you repeat the mantra with your mind. Bring your awareness to your heart. Close your eyes and listen to each mental repetition. Just allow your breathing to do what it wants." We each settled into the quiet rhythm that mantra practice brings. Like the Ganges River, this rhythm is always there. When we use a mantra we tap into it.

"Swamiji, sorry to disturb you. Swamy Nagananda is calling for you." It was Kumar.

I left Paolo and walked alone to the temple. Swamy was dressed in his yellow ochre *kashi*. He was sitting in his chair, near the larger-than-life statue of the Divine Mother Kali. I sat down and quietly continued my mantra repetitions.

Swamy asked me to open my eyes, and he looked intently into them, with a gaze of majestic power for a long minute. His sublime presence was electrifying. He was his *all* in preparation for my initiation ceremony, and speechless gratitude brought tears to my eyes.

People were coming in and out of the temple. Their activity was a backdrop of total illusion. The only reality for me at that moment was the image of Swamy Nagananda.

"I will bring you many students. You will work with them. Some will come. Some go. Some are very deep; they stay. Not important. Understand?" I nodded my head. He looked at me as if I still didn't understand.

"Everything comes from the Divine Mother. The Mother will send many to taste her divine nectar. Just let them come. Let them go. Let them stay. Whatever the Mother wants. Just talk about God. Teach others about God.

"You awaken the third eye in others. The third eye is oneness. It is where the two eyes, through meditation, disappear into one. Matter and *Atman*, or spirit are one. Understand? Body and Soul are one. You and I are one. This world and the spiritual world are one. There is only one God. There is only *Atman*."[3]

He took a deep breath, leaned forward, and as I bowed my head, he exhaled into my crown *chakra*. Then he embraced me warmly, and I asked permission for *padnamaskar*, the privilege of touching the feet of the Master to receive grace.

"Yes, yes," he said, softly and tenderly, as he stood up. I knelt, Japanese-style, in front of him on the cold stone floor, and rested my forehead on his bare feet. Unimaginable vibrations of spiritual love flowed into me, and I was fully aware of his divine stature. The moment felt like an eternity. His voice came to me softly, like music, in the distance.

"You are happy?" he asked, as a mother asks her child.

Tears streamed down my face. I couldn't answer. He laughed playfully.

"You are in the world, but no longer of it," he said.

Still kneeling with my forehead pressed to the floor, I could only hear him, and he left before I looked up. Even as he was no longer there, I could still feel his measureless affection.

The rest of the day—the final day before my initiation—was a blur of activity. Since Swamy still refused to meet with foreign visitors, he was sending them to me to answer their spiritual questions. I understood how upset he was, that so many were coming to his ashram demanding materializations from him, and offering huge sums of money to be taught the secrets of levitation and materialization. He was genuinely angry. He mocked them, did juvenile magic tricks, feigning that he was sharing "secrets," and he chased them away.

Swamy wanted people at the ashram who were genuinely seeking God and inner peace and tranquility. If all they wanted from him were his *siddhis*, he pushed them out through a variety of methods. He acted silly, like he had no knowledge of spiritual matters, playing the role of an Indian peasant who happened to acquire some land and a temple. One man came to him asking for money. Swamy materialized a fake million-dollar U.S. bill, and sent him away with it. He remained open to people who were in genuine need of healing, or who truly wanted to meditate and practice the spiritual lifestyle.

My dialogues with some of the visitors that day lasted for hours. Swamy was giving me practice in my first true *Satsangs* as Swamiji. *Satsang* is the Sanskrit word for "a meeting with a spiritual master."

I spent the entire night awake. I chose to sit upon the balcony of the wedding suite from where I could see the North Star. When I was a child, my father had taught me that I could always find my way if I could find the North Star.

A combination of factors kept me awake, the least of which were the buzzing mosquitoes, the slithering of cobras through the grass outside my balcony, and the heat. But, the truth is I wanted to stay up. Sleep didn't matter. I *couldn't* sleep. The expectation of the ceremony to come erased all fatigue.

Sitting alone in total darkness, under the warm black canopy of a star-filled sky, my entire life played out before my eyes. My mind was filled, savoring all the identities I'd passed through. It was as if each one were coming up to be reviewed and released like a series of old friends. Some brought me peace, and others drew tears that bathed my face in the moonlight.

I saw my early childhood as a motherless twin, my grade school self and the endless fist-fights with the mining town bullies. I saw the young teen sweating in the copper mine, the Eagle Scout, the financially strapped college student, and the zealous born-again Christian. I saw my medaled military years, my fellow-soldiers embracing me as their *roshi* in the Zen Buddhist tradition. I saw the martial artist, the trained runner, the bodybuilding enthusiast, the hatha yoga and meditation teacher. I saw the young married man, heading up a spiritual center, the dedicated schoolteacher, the lover, the adulterer, the mystic, the graduate student in higher education. I saw chiropractic school and the struggle to compete as an older student with a family, holding down two part-time jobs, the twice-divorced man, the broken-hearted father, the materializing Guru, the writer, the published author, the lecturer and on and on. And I was saying good-bye to all of them.

One identity I couldn't release, which was the fabric of my own Self, was my love for my soul mate Marilyn. How could I ever release my love for her? Love is the core of our existence, and the spiritual goal is to become love. This discovery can't happen in isolation. We learn who we truly are in close relationship with another person. When you are with your soul mate, you are with your Self. When you find that love, you don't release it, you *can't* release it. It is your very breath.

I felt stripped of everything but what was essential. There was nothing left of me but love: this conscious love, this divine current of love, this *prema.* This I shared with my beloved Marilyn. This pulsation of love, this reality of love defined our life.

I pondered what my world would be like after this ceremony. I already sensed how much I'd changed. Easily letting go of these thoughts and all others that entered my mind, I just kept emptying out everything that would come up. It was a deep inner cleansing that needed to take place.

As the hours passed, I realized this was all I could do to prepare myself for the coming event. Just continue to empty myself completely and become nobody...nobody special. I had to let go of all thoughts about who, or what, I thought I was, or even what I thought was happening. After many hours, there was silence.

With the arrival of the morning sun, came brilliant hues of gold, violet and orange, a revelation of color. I was so silent and so free in that moment, I could fully appreciate—as never before—the miracle of sunrise. It was birth. None of the personality traits I'd explored during the night remained. There was a notable absence of crows in this morning. It was such a new day, so pure, there was only quiet and sweetness.

A bucket of hot water was brought to the wedding suite. For the last time, I took off the white teddy bear shirt and the white slacks that had been my wardrobe during this important time of my life. I'd worn them in the presence of Babaji, and they were precious to me. I gave them a reluctant farewell. Today, for the first time in this lifetime, I was to dress in the traditional orange kashi, the sacred robe of the swamy. All the while repeating the *Om-Prema-Om* mantra, I washed carefully with soap I'd brought for the occasion from the hotel in Bangalore.

After the bath, I sat upon the cot and meditated for an hour. A group of fifty people were gathering outside my window, below the wedding suite. I was surprised by the crowd and the festive atmosphere that was developing. It was Christmas morning. I wondered why so many people were drawn to witness the ceremony. Some were foreign visitors and others were from the village. The Indian horns were being blown in the temple, and the drums played. A few people were singing sacred chants.

There was a soft knock on the door, and I heard Patrick's voice.

"Swamiji, it is almost nine o'clock. The people have come to escort you to the temple," Patrick said, with a noticeable tone of emotion. The bond between us was strong. We'd spent hours together earlier the evening before, and had become good friends. I could feel how much he cared for me that morning.

I walked slowly to the temple, where I'd been so many times before, in meditation, in my dreams, and in all the pilgrimages I'd made to Swamy in my life. On this day—like on no other—it was fully decorated with flowers. Sweet incense wafted through its halls. Inside was the local Brahmin priest, who attended all the ceremonies in the temple. There were also several musicians, sitting on the floor, playing traditional Indian instruments; drums, tambouras, vinas, horns and one harmonium.

Swamy Nagananda was standing in the front of the temple next to the large statue of the Divine Mother. He was smiling graciously, and motioned me to come inside. The temple was entirely filled with people, all sitting cross-legged on the floor.

Patrick came forward, and placed a large garland of flowers around my neck. Kumar and Dayananda threw flower petals at my feet, as I walked toward the statue of the Divine Mother and Swamy Nagananda.

Swamy stopped me just short of the entrance to the inner chamber, where the statue of Kali stood a good fifteen feet high. He reached down and picked up a lighted wick that gave off the scent of camphor. He waved it in a circular fashion, from my head to my feet three times, while reciting a blessing to the Divine Mother. Then he performed the same movement toward the statue.

"It is the Mother that gives birth. It is the Mother that brings nourishment."

Next he placed dry rice in my palm, and sprinkled it with a pinch of turmeric. He poured more rice over my head, and indicated that I offer some to Kali. I threw the rice at the statue. When my hand was empty, more rice spontaneously materialized in my palm. It just happened. I threw it again, more materialized, and I threw it as well. I could feel it as I threw it, coming directly from within my hand and oozing from my fingers. Rice is a symbol of fertility. Kali was showing me the mystery of birth, her gift of creation.

Swamy took a lighted stick of incense and performed the circular ritual again. He intoned an ancient hymn to the Divine Mother. When he finished with the incense, he turned and repeated the movement toward Kali. For me, at that moment, the Divine Mother came alive. She was alive, with only the appearance of stone. She was smiling at me compassionately, her coal-black eyes radiating a soothing fire, finally filling the void of my own mother in my life. Above her head and arms, she was haloed in a glorious light. One of her hands opened, and offered a gesture of blessing. I was astounded beyond measure as I witnessed this miracle. My body shook with uncontrollable sobs.[4]

Swamy picked up a silver cup of water. His back was to

Kali, and he seemed to be her instrument. After my realization of the night before—that I was nobody special—I saw him as an empty vessel—also a nobody—a servant of the Divine Mother. It was she who was guiding his every move through this ceremony. He placed his hand within the cup, while reciting sacred mantras, then sprinkled some of the perfumed holy water upon my head. When he finished he offered the water to Kali.

"You already have blessings of the Divine Father. Now you have full protection of the Divine Mother." The knowing had been imparted to me through the ritual, but I was touched by his verbal confirmation.

Swamy tied an orange silk sash over my right shoulder like a sling. It encircled my left arm, and hung at my side.

"This is symbol of your worldly possessions. It may seem to others that you own many things. You own nothing. You no longer belong to the world and yet the whole world will belong to you. Now you, and everything you have, belong to the Mother. Mother will bring you always what you need. Kali will spread your name wide and far. Trust in the Mother."

Through my tears, I smiled gratefully at my Guru, and bowed my head with reverence as I remained silent. There were no words.

"You have come before the Mother with just your heart. I asked you to come empty...with nothing, so that the Mother could fill you with her gifts. You will have many new discoveries. Many students will come to you."

Swamy leaned forward, and whispered a deep truth with many facets into my ear. It was priceless. I felt immeasurably uplifted. He had given me a passport to Heaven.

Aloud, he said, "Remember always, God is simple. Everything else is complex."

His eyes twinkled. At this time, there was the blinding flash of several cameras. Still, I was silent. I could only look at Swamy, and nod when appropriate. He whispered my swamy name into my ear.

"*Swamiji*," he said aloud, with a gentle voice.

"Prema Baba Swamiji," I said silently to myself, repeating my name for the first time. With so much going on, I wanted to make sure I wouldn't forget it.

He came forward, gazed deep into my eyes, and then embraced me.

"You will awaken others to God through your eyes," he said. "Your look and touch will heal others and bring blessings." We held onto each other for a long time.

"It is the custom that you must now give your blessings to these people," he said, stepping back, and taking control of the flow of events. "They have come for your blessings. Your whole life is to give blessings. It is your duty. But first you must give your blessing to the Mother."

I turned to face Kali. She was looking at me. This was definitely not a mere statue. It was alive. It was the Divine Mother in living form. My empty right hand involuntarily flew back into the air with a whip-like motion, as if catching a baseball. Then it flew forward, as a cloud of *vibhuti* left my hand to land gently upon the goddess.

I reverently spoke my first words as a swamy to Kali.

"*Kali Ma*," I whispered.

My hand automatically shot back a second time, and came forward again to release more *vibhuti*.

"For Marilyn, my beloved."

I whispered these words. My prayer, my first blessing as a swamy, was for her bliss, her spiritual realization, and to know that we would never be apart.

I was about to turn toward the crowd when my hand shot backward a third time, and came forward again releasing another cloud of holy ash.

"For Lisa." My thoughts at that moment were a prayer for Kali to bring joy and bliss to my divine daughter.

Swamy turned me to look into the sea of radiant, joyous faces. As soon as I faced them, they bowed. I returned the bow to them. Then, I moved among the sweet people—a servant of the Divine Mother Kali and the Father Babaji—touching babies, mothers, grandmothers, fathers, brothers, sisters, and grandfathers.

The crowd followed as Swamy led me outside the temple to the very spot where I'd sat meditating in my boyhood dreams, and where I first stood when I recognized him as my lifelong guide.

Swamy was laughing merrily.

"You will be a married swamy," he said. "I brought you and Marilyn together, and nothing can separate you."

I'd never doubted it. I wouldn't have gone forward with this ceremony if it meant leaving my sacred marriage behind.

"The West needs balanced approach to spirituality," Swamy added. "They need the male and female, the Mother and the Father. I have one more gift to give."

Again he whispered into my ear. This final blessing of the ceremony would remain my secret prophecy. It was time for me to leave. I was being instructed to return to the West, and to bring the blessings of the Swamy Order to the millions of sweet souls thirsting for enlightenment.

The crowd escorted me to the white Ambassador, parked outside the ashram. Babu was dressed up today, and wearing sunglasses. He had been my photographer during the ceremony, and he was in full celebration mode. He took my luggage from Patrick, and put it in the trunk. The crowd gathered in closely, wanting further blessings. It was difficult to get into the car. Part of me wanted to stay, and hang onto this moment forever, but I knew it was time to go.

Babu started the car, and I had one foot inside. I held onto the door, and looked toward the temple one last time. A solitary white flag waved in the breeze above its turret. I'd not noticed it before. There is always something new to see in every moment.

Swamy was still standing on the spot where I'd first recognized him. We waved at each other and I bowed my head and clasped my hands in *Namaste*. My heart overflowed with gratitude. My eyes took in the lush green hills, the brilliance of the warm Indian sun, my beloved Guru Swamy Nagananda—splendid in orange *kashi*, the color vivid against the white of the ashram walls.

"When will I see this place again?" I wondered.

I pulled myself into the cab, and settled cross-legged in the center of the seat. I was in a state of happy tranquility. Everything was perfect. As the Ambassador slowly rolled off, the crowd shot off a series of firecrackers that punctuated the silence, and actually increased it by contrast.

"Happy birthday, Swamiji!" Babu greeted me with love.

I couldn't speak.

"Thank you, Babu," I finally whispered.

That night I would catch a flight to Bombay. In Bombay I would take another flight to Frankfurt, Germany, where I would meet my darling Marilyn. I was counting the minutes until our reunion.

"We go to Bangalore now," I said.

"Is it far to Bangalore, sir?" Babu asked. He was laughing. I was in deep meditation with my eyes open. I didn't respond. I couldn't find any words. From my heart, I could hear Babaji's voice, in sing-song melody, "*Leela. Watch the Leela.*"

"Swamiji, is it *far*?" Babu reiterated. He looked at me with an expression of longing that said he was asking about the spiritual realm of *Premananda* where I now resided.

"No, it's not far," I said softly.

ENDNOTES

BABAJI

[1] Paramhansa Yogananda, *Autobiography of a Yogi*, Chapter 33, *Babaji, the Yogi-Christ of Modern India*, pp. 290–310, Crystal Clarity Publishers, Nevada City, CA, First Printing, 1946.

[2] The ancient symbol of the swastika represents that God's energy flows in every direction. It was for thousands of years a spiritual symbol before it became the symbol of Nazism. The Hindu symbol is not identical to the Nazi swastika.

[3] Mary Magdalene was married to Jesus, and she was a powerful influence on his work. It was at the Council of Trent in the fifth century that her status was reduced to that of a prostitute to elevate the patriarchal God and stamp out the Goddess.

[4] The Sanskrit word for wind, which simultaneously means *prana*.

[5] The five-thousand-year-old tale of Krishna's dialogue with Arjuna on the battlefield of Kurushetra, a metaphor for humanity's struggle with the inner demons and its transcendence.

[6] The chakras are spiritual body vortices or power centers.

[7] The silver cord is mentioned in Ecclesiastes 12:6: "Or ever the silver cord be loosed or the golden bowl be broken, or the pitcher be broken at the fountain, or the wheel be broken at the cistern."

[8] According to the Hatha Yoga master Iyengar, the *khanda* is an egg-shaped nerve bulb located two inches below the navel within the spiritual body. Some traditions state that our entire 72,000 nerves or nadis originate from the *khanda*. When the *khanda* is purified through Khanda breathing, scars of past lives are removed. In Zen Buddhism, the khanda is the *hara*—long respected in Asian cultures and martial arts as the center and source of power.

[9] The traditional spiritual greeting in India. The hands are in prayer fashion and the head is bowed.

[10] A brown bead made from the multifaceted seed of the sacred *rudraksha* tree. They are worn and cherished as spiritual power beads.

[11] The cloth wrap-like diaper popularized through images of Ghandi.

[12] Sanskrit word for a holy vision of the divine one.

[13] Krishna's main disciple in the Bhagavad Gita.

[14] Bhakti is the path of pure love.

[15] Babaji always pronounced it "Christ-nah."

[16] *Rishis* were wise men of another era.

[17] The written Hindu spiritual legacy, which is encyclopedic in length, was originally passed down orally.

[18] A bow of respect, usually on the knees with the head to the ground.

[19] Mantras are sacred sounds and phrases designed by the ancient rishis to lead one to God realization.

PETALS FROM THE LOTUS

[1] The burning of *karma* is referred to by *yogis* as "cooking." They further say as you grow spiritually, you are "baking." Remember, the term *Siddha* means "cooked."

INITIATION

[1] The Hindu goddess, a symbol of God and the aspect of the eternal Mother Nature. She is traditionally depicted as a four-armed woman standing on the god Shiva, or the Infinite. Four arms symbolize cardinal attributes of creation and destruction.

[2] A *Japamala* is a strand of *rudraksha*, sandalwood, or other sacred wood or stone beads. It is of varying lengths of 108, 54, or 27 beads strung together, and used, depending on its length, as a prayer necklace or bracelet. It is similar to a Catholic rosary.

[3] Swamy often said things that could be contradicted by logic, but his purpose was always to stop the mind's activity, so he could take me to the transcendental realms of truth. This teaching he was giving me was so important, and I knew it contradicted many New Age teachings. We are told we are bodies that have spirits, or spirits that have bodies. What Swamy was saying is it's all spirit. When we look at each other, we're looking at spirit. Matter and spirit are the same.

[4] Ramakrishna, India's famous *Avatar* of the last century, once saw Kali move after praying to her devotedly in a temple in Calcutta. He wasn't alone. Many had seen this symbol of feminine creation come to life.